For Kathleen,
    with my love always.
                Mary

Barbon,
Christmas, 1966.

PAGEANT OF LAKELAND

A. H. GRIFFIN

PAGEANT OF LAKELAND

The Changing Year in the Fell Country

There are no hills like the Wasdale hills
When Spring comes up the dale,
Nor any woods like the larch woods
Where the primroses blow pale;
And the shadows flicker quiet-wise
On the stark ridge of Black Sail.

Anon.

Photograghs by G. V. Berry

ROBERT HALE · LONDON

PRINTED IN GREAT BRITAIN
BY EBENEZER BAYLIS AND SON, LIMITED
THE TRINITY PRESS, WORCESTER, AND LONDON

CONTENTS

ILLUSTRATIONS

ACKNOWLEDGEMENT

All the above photographs were specially taken
for this book by G. V. Berry of Kendal.

FOREWORD

THERE is no best time for seeing Lakeland. Any month can be as rewarding as another, in a different sort of way. For myself, I especially enjoy the winter months with the holiday crowds departed, the hills transformed and heightened by the snows and the views long and clear. Selfishly, as the summer bustle nears its end I tend to await quieter roads and less crowded mountain sides with increasing impatience, and the sight of the first snows seems to compensate for days of mist and rain. But spring is a time of real magic in Lakeland and autumn a most beautiful interlude between the full-blown glories of summer and the sharp, fresh tang of winter.

To know Lakeland, therefore, one must see it in all seasons, and this book is an attempt at a portrait of the district—an outdoors picture—throughout each month of the year. It is not the story or the thoughts around one particular year but a sort of distillation of a great many of them, backed by a lifetime's love of the area. The background to the book has been between four and five hundred of my "Country Diary" notes from *The Guardian* spread over sixteen years which have enabled me to have some sort of record of wanderings and observations that otherwise might have been forgotten. At least half of these scribblings have been rejected, but the remainder have been completely re-written, extended, compressed, turned inside out and edited, together with more than their weight of new matter, into what I hope is a fairly homogenous whole. And to Alastair Hetherington, the Editor of *The Guardian* and himself a man of the hills, I wish to express my gratitude for many years of encouragement and for his ready support of this latest venture.

Some readers may notice that the book may be slanted slightly towards Westmorland since more of my writing is around the county in which I live. But my affection could be even stronger for some of the Cumberland—and Lancashire—parts of the National Park and, where appropriate, I have dealt with the western dales and other places, including even the Northern Pennines, where my wanderings might have taken me. For although I see the Westmorland hills every day and places like Windermere and Grasmere every week, either Wasdale Head or Coniston could be my spiritual home.

I would also like to thank G. V. Berry of Kendal for providing the excellent pictures which illustrate this book and my wife for her invaluable help with typing and proof reading and her patience with a husband who tends to neglect both house and garden when the mountains call.

A.H.G.

Cunswick End
Kendal
May 1966

A PROLOGUE

THE Lake District embraces the most exciting, lovely and varied scenery in England. Here are the highest mountains in the country and the deepest lakes, quiet green valleys threaded by rippling trout streams, rock-girt pools set like jewels among the crags, and dancing becks and waterfalls leaping down the fellsides. Low stone-built farmhouses nestle down in folds among the bracken and heather, pleasant old-world villages dot the district, and stone walls, centuries old, zigzag—higgledy-piggledy—over the skyline. And the mountain sheep, grey-faced and sorrowful, wander across the fells.

It is a countryside that changes every day and no matter how long one has lived here there is always something new to see and to learn. Even in a lifetime you cannot know the whole. I have the great good fortune to live just inside the National Park and from my windows look out every day on the familiar skyline of friendly mountains. As often as possible I get into the hills and crags, and for many years I have been trying to chronicle the life of the countryside. Each month brings new activities and interests in and around the dales and every day the hills look different.

There is no "proper" time of the year to visit the Lake District, and unless the picture is seen during all months of the year, in fair weather and foul, it will be incomplete. And so, in the pages that follow, I have tried to trace some of the high-lights—as well as some of the little things—of one man's outdoor Lakeland year. Perhaps it may give at least a peep at the whole picture.

For my Mother
for her Encouragement

1

SUNLIGHT AND SNOW
January

THE first month of the year, with the Christmas cards just taken down off the mantelpiece and the withered holly branches thrown on the fire, is the time in Lakeland for the young, the fit and all who prefer the magic stillness of winter to the summer clamour and crowds. A quiet month, just before the first shy snowdrops break through, when the fell country is in its deepest sleep, but sometimes, too, a month when the elements up above may be very much awake. A dramatic month outdoors, therefore, and often a very beautiful month indeed. True, there may be rain or fog at times but most Lakeland Januarys produce many days of sunshine on the snows—cold, crisp days with the tarns, and perhaps even the lakes themselves, frozen hard, and bracing winds on the heights.

And so the energetic go out into the hills to walk, climb or ski, or try out their skating skills, or to follow the foxhounds across the fells. This, too, is often the month for the ploughing competitions and the tests for walling and hedging so that, if the east winds are not too bitter, there are excuses enough to wrap up well and get outdoors. And the compensations for making the effort, apart from the new feeling of well-being and glowing cheeks, can be rewarding enough—the mountains, more impressive than at any other time of the year; the red-coated huntsman striding up the lane with his hounds towards the fells on a frosty morning; a sunset high up among the snows, or moonlight on a frozen mere and, in the evenings, the great joy of a hot bath and food and drink before a blazing log fire.

The beginning of 1962 was the most perfect outdoor turn of the year within most of our memories with skating over Christmas, ski-ing over New Year, and something like a fortnight of long, crisp, sunny days. Even water-ski-ing on Windermere on Christmas Day. And not the usual English snow and ice—either wet and sloppy or wrinkled and blotchy—but the sort of unconsolidated snow we pray for in Switzerland, dry and floury to fall into, and smooth, black ice calling for the sharpest blades. But the great phenomenon was the exceptional clarity of the skies and the long hours of unbroken sunshine, strong enough at times—if you picked your spot—to get yourself sunburned. Two memories out of many will long be treasured—Christmas Day on frozen Tarn Hows, and a short, stolen hour on New Year's Day on a little snow-capped hill near Kendal looking out over half the Lake District. We ate our pork sandwiches and mince pies, I remember, washed down with half a bottle of Christmas wine, as we sat in the sunshine among the trees, resting from our exertions on the ice. Towards evening the fells that encircle these superbly sited mountain pools turned purple, the western sky behind them glowed orange and then flamed with gold, and a great, frosty silence came down and gripped the earth in its iron fist until the bright sunlight of the morning. And from the little snow hill on the first day of the year I saw thirty peaks stretched out along the horizon like fairy castles in icing sugar, each one sparkling and glinting in the afternoon sun.

The great thing about snow on the fells is that it makes the views so much better. A tremendous depth is not required. Even a modest covering will cause the crags to emerge from hiding and stand out boldly, black and stark, against the white slopes, throwing their blue shadows across the snow. One ideal weather combination is bright intermittent sunlight in the late afternoon an hour or so before the sunset over the sea, with a fair amount of changing cloud, perhaps recent rain in the valleys to bring out the glints in the rock, and a strong wind for varying the cloud shadows and whipping the snow off the cornices. Snow on the fells can reflect the lighting in an almost fantastic way. Distant crags that on other days may look dull and colourless stand out blue, remote, and seemingly twice their real height when there is the right amount of snow about, and on occasions can look like weird formations in a bleak, Arctic landscape. If there is snow on the fells, and you are in the right position, a shaft of sunlight can illuminate a featureless green valley, in contrast with the whiteness above, until it looks like a magic corridor of gold, and the sun can gild summit rocks set among the snows until they might be on fire. And the tarns, in days of snow, sunshine, and shadow, take on a fairy quality that can be almost unbelievable so that an ordinary dull sheet of water can become a magical splash of ultramarine, turquoise, or the warm, deep red of rich wine seen in candlelight.

On one of these exciting days I went up into the hills to think out an article. So much easier to think, alone in the mountains, when the only problems are of wind and muscle. Most of the country, I remember, was either shrouded in fog or swept by snow blizzards but in Lakeland, despite the usual unenthusiastic weather forecasts the sun shone down out of an almost cloudless sky. And, even at nearly 3,000 feet, the air remained so still that tobacco smoke rose straight in the air, and hovered there. Indeed, the loneliest summits must have been among the quietest places in England. A rock-hard frost gripped all the mountains in its claws so that the becks were stilled, the birds absent or silent, and the grass, through which a breeze might sigh, hidden deep beneath the frozen snows. Not even a distant slither of scree or the splash of a waterfall. Just a silent, white world. From Fairfield I looked down over half the fell country and far beyond, across to the Helvellyn ridges plastered in ice and the white, pointed peak of Catstye Cam probing the sky, away to the reaches of Ullswater hidden in a shimmer of floating mists, and the orange and brown of Patterdale, and, distantly, to the white wall of the Northern Pennines stretched along the eastern horizon. And later as the shadows lengthened across the snow I watched, in the opposite heavens the pageantry of the sunset. Gradually the western hills turned purple, the great ball of the sun dropped down in a blaze of orange and gold behind the Buttermere fells, and night crept down over the mountains.

One of the first places to freeze in our part of the world is

Ratherheath Tarn, which nestles in the woods about three miles north-west of Kendal. Tarn Hows near Coniston freezes early too and Rydal Water is generally the first of the lakes to freeze. But many a winter goes by without even a skimming over the bays in Windermere. In January 1963 the ice was rippled and pockmarked on Ratherheath, but beyond the rushes on Rydal Water a few miles away it was smooth and black. Our blades sang as they cut the ice and the crisp air reddened our cheeks, but the principal glory was of the western sky, aflame with an incredible sunset behind the purple outline of the fells, and later, of a glorious moon shining down on the silvered ice and a stilled countryside. One of the many perfect winter days that year, so beautiful that the wireless news seemed to be of another world. Sometimes the east winds were bitter and the snow clouds menacing, but, sandwiched between them were still, sunlit days with skies of poster blue and distant, snow-capped hills that seemed suddenly to have leaped into the foreground. Every day from my house I could see, away to the north-east, the long line of the smoothly sculptured Howgill fells—we used to think they looked like sleeping elephants—snowbound, top to toe, for weeks, and, to the north-west, the wild trough of Kentmere winding deep into craggy mountains. This day, home again from Rydal, there were only two colours in the distant scene—dazzling white and shadowed blue—but in the foreground there was welcome warmth in the rich browns of stately, old trees, and the weathered grey of sun-splashed farm buildings. Two men were hard at work down the lane sawing an old tree for winter logs, and the shrill whirr of the saw was the only sound in a quiet, frozen countryside.

There was one January day in 1959 when you could walk on the ice right across Windermere just north of the ferry for the first time since the well-remembered 1947 winter. The first and the last time I skated on England's longest lake was in 1929, when the ice was several inches thick and hundreds of cars were parked on it. I remember cycling there as a youth and skating northwards up the lake for two or three miles. There were braziers on the ice to keep the skaters warm, refreshment stalls, and dense crowds of people. One old Ambleside resident Mr. Lovell Mason who has been skating in Lakeland for more than eighty years and was again the first man on Rydal Water in

Companion of the Hills

1959 clearly remembers being taken on the ice on Windermere in either 1879 or 1880. In his opinion the finest Lakeland winter for skaters was 1895, when the lake was frozen for six weeks and well into March. Coaches were driven across the ice and from all parts of the country people flocked to Lakeland for the skating. There were even railway excursions from London, and sometimes the ice was packed with thousands of people. They said the ice was eighteen inches thick, but at night the people of Ambleside could hear it roaring and cracking as it settled down on the water, until finally it broke right across the lake and a man went through the gap and was drowned.

The best ploughs in the country, they say, used to come from Westmorland—and some of the best ploughmen, too. How strange, therefore, that competitive ploughing has now almost disappeared from the county. Only one society remains, but there are no horses at the annual competitions—only tractors. And the best ploughmen are the best mechanics. But although ploughing today is no longer the skilful handling of a pair of horses but rather the expert setting of a confusion of levers, a good furrow can still be a thing of beauty. Every countryman thinks he knows a good furrow when he sees one and we all get our eyes down to the ground and check the furrows for straightness when the competitions come round, but the neatest-looking furrow does not necessarily win first prize. The sort of grassland furrow the judges are looking for in the north nowadays is nothing like the pointed affair with almost a curl on top that was most favoured in years gone by. Instead, the ideal furrow today is much more rounded, and, on stubble land, almost squarish and rather more broken. But all good furrows should be straight, closed packed, even and level, with each one identical with its neighbour, no indication of where the ploughing started, and a shallow finish. Horse ploughing may have almost disappeared but the tractor-man on the skyline making quick, new patterns on his tilted fields, and the hungry gulls wheeling overhead, is still one of the grandest sights of the countryside.

One old waller at the competitions sometimes held with the ploughing matches, his grimy hands bare to the biting wind, knelt in the snow, surveyed with pride his new, dry-stone wall,

2

Great How Crags from Brim Fell
Skating on Ratherheath Tarn

already three feet high and told me: "All ye've git to do is find t'feeace o' t' steean and then fit it in, but happen it's nut ivvery fool as can find it.' He then carefully selected a stone from the heap of most unlikely-looking material at his side, dexterously chipped a fragment off one corner, placed it in position, and leaned back to assess the result. I noted later that he had picked up the first prize.

The ancient Lake District craft of dry-stone walling has been having something of a revival in recent years, and competition is still keen at the village walling contests. Sometimes you will see youngsters, as young as ten or twelve, rushing up short sections of dry-stone wall with a skill and dash suggesting they had spent the whole of their short lives doing just this and nothing else. Having on occasions tried my hand at repairing tumbledown garden walls and never achieving anything better than a tottering pile that collapsed the following winter, I know something of the hidden pitfalls in this job, but these nippers make it look easier than shovelling coal. They seem to know at a glance which stone from their pile of irregularly shaped rocks is the one to put in next, and when they have to do a bit of chipping with their hammers they toss the stone about in their hands as other folk might examine a golf ball. The walls they build for the judges will last a long time, for these lads' forbears built the hundreds of miles of walls marching over the fells that in places have stood up to mountain weather for more than a hundred years.

The very oldest of the stone walls zigzagging up the fell-sides may be nearly a thousand years old. All of them are boundaries of one sort or another—fences between farms, parish or county boundaries, enclosures around manors or commons, and so on—and all the hundreds of miles of them have been built, slowly and with great labour, by craftsmen. Anybody can run up some sort of a dry-stone wall but ten to one it will come down after the first frost or gales; it takes skill to build, without mortar, a wall that will stand up to the on-slaughts of wind and rain, frost and snow, for a hundred years or more. Less than a century ago these wall builders worked twelve hours a day for a weekly wage of seven and sixpence. Often they had no time, or daylight, to get down to the valley to sleep and had to camp out on the spot. They built walls—

finding their stone as they went along—four feet six inches high, two feet six inches thick at the base and a foot less at the top. Each man had to build seven yards of wall a day—or starve.

Many of my adventures in the hills are with my Border collie, Sambo, an affectionate old fellow, too lazy to work sheep, but always glad for a walk over the tops. He has a splendid white waistcoat, white feet, a curious domed head, an odd pink patch above his nose that gives him a lopsided look, and a bare patch at the top of his bushy tail, caused through getting too close to the fire. He has a stitched wound in one paw, still showing, where he was kicked by a cow and many old scars that are the legacies of battles with other dogs. Every time I take him to Scotland he seems to get mauled, but he is really the most patient and long-suffering animal I have ever had, and will quietly submit to any indignity upon his person by one of the family. He has only won one battle that I know of—a fight with a fierce Alsatian that ended, remarkably, with Sambo biting off a small portion of his attacker's nose. I have never bothered to list Sambo's ascents, but he has certainly been to the top of almost every mountain in Lakeland and has also been hauled in rope slings up several moderate rock climbs. He always knows when I'm going out and can hardly contain himself when he sees me getting out rucksack or boots. But, by the end of a long day he is tired out and curls up in the back of the car, dead to the world.

One balmy January day, with the ground softening fast and the ice on the skating ponds turning to water, Sambo and I went into the hills for some badly needed exercise. In the valley I remember noticing the wood-smoke from the cottage chimneys rising straight upwards without a waver, and it was quite warm enough for shirt sleeves in the morning sunlight. But on the top you could almost lean on the wind, and the freezing cold crept through thick sweaters and anorak and bit at cheeks and fingers. Rocks were completely glazed in ice and hung with fingers of frost—sometimes as if a barrow load of feathers had been tipped over them—and everywhere the snow was rock hard. Only rarely are conditions so arctic as this in Lakeland.

One snowdrift where we often ski—Savage's Drift on Raise—was frozen so hard that its direct ascent needed an ice axe, and I was so immersed in the work that I failed to notice, until I had almost reached the top, that Sambo, whose pads normally grip better than vibrams,[1] was no longer with me. Looking down, I spotted him slowly picking his way up from the bottom of the slope, a few hundred feet below, and was told by the only other person on that part of the mountain at the time that he had seen the dog slide most of the way down the gully on his back. But Sambo was none the worse for his adventure and cheerfully led with the same determination on to the snow-plastered summit of White Side as if to show that it wouldn't happen again. The view from the ice-locked cairn was tremendous—the valleys aglow with a rich orange light, the peaks capped with snow and, between them, peeps into Scotland and over to Cross Fell.

On another day Sambo and I went into the Northern Pennines beyond Appleby where I hoped to find snow for an afternoon's ski-ing. Down in the valley it had been a quiet morning, with gulls wheeling above the stubble fields, the sun glowing on the red sandstone walls in the lane and not a sign of snow. But up on the summit we might have been at the South Pole. Visibility was down to a few yards, a fierce wind flayed my cheeks, and the snow had drifted deep enough in places to bury a standing man. Icicles hanging from the eyebrows were nearly as much of a nuisance as the driving snow and Sambo was soon completely plastered in snow and ice with just two little dark specks to show where his eyes were. But the hard exercise kept us warm, and my inability to see whether the slope went up or down a few feet beyond my ski points gave me plenty to think about. Several times the dog disappeared as suddenly and completely as if he had dived into a pool and more than once I did much the same thing. It was darkening quickly when we left the summit, the dog floundering along behind me, but the snow had stopped by the time we reached the mountain road that dipped down, a winding white ribbon, towards the village. Gratefully, I pointed my skis down the middle of it and sailed effortlessly and silently down the mountainside.

Our ski hut stands exactly on the 2,500-feet contour in the Helvellyn range but nestles so cleverly into the mountainside that you might pass within fifty yards and never spot it. It is probably the highest mountain hut in England and was

[1] Moulded rubber soles.

completed after six months of week-end volunteer labour. Planning approval for new buildings high up in the fells is rarely given, but this neat affair of cedarwood mounted on a plinth of local stone is so innocuous and so remote from any skyline view that consent was readily forthcoming. There is no sleeping there—just a week-end refuge from the icy winds and a first-aid centre for injured skiers. A little Christmas tree was once planted near the entrance but it failed to survive the gales. But the hut, lashed down with steel cables, can ride out any storm and the cedarwood is nicely weathering into the colour of the mountainside, so that the little shelter seems to be disappearing even further into the rocks and steep grass of one of the least frequented corners of the Lake District.

Most Januarys bring several opportunities for ski-ing on the fells—short hours hastily snatched from a workaday week which is the way to enjoy ski-ing in Lakeland. You must seize your opportunities when you can, for if you wait for ideal conditions you may never get out at all. Sometimes I have been able to manage an odd hour in the fields at the back of my house, while another day an hour's indifferent ski-ing might involve a thirty-miles drive in the rain, followed by a trudge through the mist to the mountain tops. But one short January day was enjoyed only a few miles from Kendal along the Sedbergh road—a perfect winter's day of hard frost, bright sunshine, and tremendous Alpine views. We drove along the crackling snow ruts, up a long, winding hill, and, on the edge of the fells, snapped on our skis. The snow, nicely crusted and just deep enough to cover the tussocks of heather, sparkled and winked at us as we slid noise-lessly down the hillside, and a handful of Swaledales, nosing for the grass, didn't even bother to look up as we skimmed past. When we were back at the top again for a second run the view had even improved. The late afternoon sun had sunk well down towards the sea, making the whole of the western sky a bright backcloth of gold flecked with dusty grey clouds like oversize gun bursts. The Kent estuary, many miles away, danced in the distant sunshine, the slim, stately larches idly flicked the snow from their finger-tips, and the old grey town lay smoking in the valley at our feet. Behind us, the great fells, looking three times their height, stood deeply plastered in snow so thick that even the crags were hidden.

A sudden glint of sunlight burnished the rich colours of an old barn, until then just a dark shape against the snow, and a pair of whooper swans, visitors from Iceland looking for a winter home, sailed low over the fields. Half an hour later a fine half-moon, with a single star at her foot for company, shone out on a crisp, white world.

There was another stolen hour on the low fells below Kirkstone Pass. Swiftly and silently we swooped in great curves down the lower slopes and through the larches to the road and slipped out of our ski bindings by the dry-stone wall that circles the farm. It was pleasant to stand upright in the snow for a few moments and, before trudging down to the car, to peep over the old wall and see how John's lambing ewes were getting on. There were only about a dozen, all black-faced Rough Fells—the mountain sheep of Westmorland—and against the snow they looked rather like dark boulders somehow missed by the storm. Hard as we stared we could see no movement from any of them for each one was quietly cropping from a square foot of grass at the bottom of the little hole she had dug for herself in the snow. But all over the field, criss-crossed like railway lines at a busy junction, were the little hoof-prints of their wanderings and, at the end of each perfectly straight line, the tell-tale cave in the snow. If snow came down harder that evening, I thought, these would be the shelters where the sheep would spend the night, and even if they were "overblown" it would be warm and cosy inside. John's expectant mothers would take no harm.

On one of the first days of 1965 two of us went for a walk over Helvellyn—the tourists' mountain. In the valley the ground was rock hard, long icicles hung over Grisedale Beck, and there was a very raw wind blowing out of the west. The tops were hidden behind dark grey clouds and out of the murk long slivers of snow reached down into the dale. Half-way up the fell a thin floury snowfall turned into a mild blizzard and visibility shortened to a few yards, so that although we knew that Red Tarn lay far below us to the right and the mountain straight ahead we could see neither. Nothing but snow at our feet, the plastered rocks immediately ahead, and all around us the wind swirling the flakes into a fury.

Balancing along the topmost rocks of Striding Edge proved an interesting problem for having decided to take a step during a temporary lull one was nearly always caught by a fresh gust exactly at the wrong moment. The climb up the front of Helvellyn was easy, however, and the cornice quickly negotiated with just a few scrapes from the ice axe. But the "white-out" on top was complete, the memorial to Gough's faithful dog hardly visible from two yards away and the so-called shelter covered over with drifted snow. There seemed little point in idling on the summit for it was difficult to remain upright and not easy even to see, although I discovered later that vision was being impeded by long icicles hanging from the eyebrows. So honour having been satisfied on such a wild day we turned down the rocks of Swirral Edge and kicked and slithered our way down to the valley and the splendid luxury of hot baths. We had seen nobody in the hills all afternoon—not even a footprint in the snow.

A January morning drive over the snowbound fells to the little county assize town of Appleby was a delight, although the icy road with its sweeping curves required most of my attention. The sun sparkled on a white world of rolling moors and smiling fells, and the only people seen on the twenty-five-mile run were two or three roadmen, muffled over the ears with Balaclavas or motor-cycle helmets. They were spending the morning shovelling grit on to the slippiest places and stamping about to keep themselves warm. Now and again I nearly ran into sheep that had escaped from the fields and were trotting across the roadway or feeding in the hedgerows, always just at the iciest places. Over Orton Scar the wind had blown the snow off the road so that it wandered like a dark wavy line through the whiteness towards the Pennines. An angry sky over to the east suggested more snow that night but you could see quite clearly the radar masts on the summit of Great Dun Fell, several miles away, glinting in the sunlight. As I bumped over the frozen ruts into the little tree-lined town the assize trumpeters in their regalia were standing in the snow, sounding a fanfare for the judge. Then the great man, an imposing figure in full-bottomed wig and robes of red, smiling in acknowledgement of the saluting policemen and respectful locals, stepped into the courthouse, and dignity had descended again on a tiny town.

And I remember another journey to Appleby a few days later. For half the distance I crawled, sidelights switched on, through a gloomy white world with visibility about the length of a cricket pitch, but when I came out of the gorge near Tebay the day suddenly changed. First, a patch of blue sky appeared in the windscreen, and a moment later I had driven out of the swirling fog into glorious sunlight, with wonderfully clear views over the Scar to the Pennines. It was just like emerging from a black smoke-filled tunnel into the open country. Through the rear window I could see the ragged northern edge of the great fog belt, sprawling like a huge, unclean monster over the country-side, with its farthest tentacles feeling along the bonniest trout stream in the district. Ahead, the morning sun glinting on old stone walls and hardly a cloud in the sky.

Before heavy rains and driving clouds blotted out the hills we snatched a short winter's day on the tops above Longsleddale. At noon we passed an old man repairing a stretch of dry-stone wall, but did not see another soul until we drove down the lane in the evening. The lights of the car picked out the lost rem-nants of a hunt in the shape of a farmer's lad with a couple of weary-looking hounds at heel, on their way to a warm supper. The only other living things we saw all day were the sheep cropping the frozen mountain herbs and a pair of ravens wheel-ing above the head of the valley. The pools in the winding track over the pass were iced over, and there were fingers of snow every few yards. Convoys of laden pack-horses used to zig-zag this way through the fells, but the only imprints we saw was an occasional half-moon of climbers' nails. It was biting cold on top and the wind, sweeping from the gaunt fells to the north-east, nearly took one's breath away. The snow on the summit ridge was as hard as rock, heavily scored by the wind, and embel-lished here and there with little spillikins of ice that broke off under our feet and went tinkling down the frozen slopes in a delightful diminuendo of fairy music.

It was a relief to swing south at the cairn on Harter Fell, feel the wind at one's back for a change, and admire the view in comfort. The Pennines were hidden in a storm brewing up over there, but far to the south the flat top of Ingleborough was unmistakable, while ten miles away the roofs of Kendal were hidden under a blanket of mist and fog with only the castle ruins peeping up above the gloom.

One January we found ourselves, quite suddenly, in the midst of the worst floods for years. The previous morning we had awakened to a white world, the snow inches thick on the lawns and in deep drifts on the passes, but within hours the country-side had been transformed. The River Kent, one of the fastest flowing in England, went racing through Kendal that afternoon in a relentless brown torrent, bearing with it great trees, hen-house roofs, and oil drums, besides many, many millions of tons of melted snow from the fells. People in the riverside houses, anxiously watching the rising waters all day, began bringing up their valuables out of the cellars and taking up the carpets in the lower rooms. Some of them remembered the last time, when the kitchen table floated underneath the ceiling. A little way out of the town the roads were flooded right across in places, and acres of fields were under water. Trees, fences, and telegraph poles were growing out of the floods, and the sheep and cattle huddled together, rather sorrowful-looking, on tiny islands. That evening the angry river, churning and boiling in its brown fury, swirled across the roadway into the first cellars and it was an anxious and busy night for many, but next morning things were back to normal again. A few carpets hanging out to dry seemed the only evidence of the floods and the river-side dwellers could forget their fears for a time.

Floods, blizzards, and gales made a dramatic start to 1965 after three big floods the previous month. Who would have thought, with the latest floods barely subsided and the fields still waterlogged, that we would get snow, and that it would stick? And yet, while in Kendal we were looking out at curtains of driving sleet, lorries were bogged down in snow on Shap Fells only a few miles away and roadmen were out all night in the blizzard trying to get the traffic moving again. And it wasn't only the snow that was blocking the road, the gales were also doing their share. During one alarming night at least forty trees—some of them quite large—were blown down across Westmorland roads so that if you managed to get over the high passes without running into a snow drift or jammed behind a long line of blocked lorries you still stood a good chance of being held up on lower ground by fallen trees. You could see the wind whipping the new snow on the mountains into clouds, blowing it off the west slopes and dropping it down on the eastern sides. Meanwhile the lower fells were alive with new becks splashing down to the roads and one of the most dramatic sights of the week was that of 400 million gallons of Manchester's water spilling to waste in one day over the Haweswater dam.

The holiday visitors loudly proclaiming that fox-hunting was cruel and ought to be stopped did not know the short, sturdy dalesman in gaiters sitting quietly at the back of the smoke-room one January evening was one of the best-known huntsmen in the Lake District, and just then something of a local celebrity. After a hard day on the tops in wild weather Joe Wear did not propose to waste his breath in explanation or argument, but when the noisy visitors had departed he modestly acknowledged our congratulations on his record half-season's hunting. Never before had his mountain pack—the Ullswater—killed more than thirty foxes up to the turn of the year, but so far that season his hounds had accounted for forty-seven, including nine in one week.

Joe was amused when he recalled that the visitors had suggested shooting when told that Lake District foxes had to be kept down if the poultry and young lambs had to be protected. Often enough his hounds comb the fells all day and never put up a fox, and a man would be fortunate indeed to get the chance of a shot in the hills. Waiting with a gun outside the fowlhouse for a marauding Christmas fox believed to be in the area is another matter, and some are killed in this way. On the fells Reynard might be wounded by shooting and crawl into a borran to die a lingering death. But at the end of a long, wild chase over the tops the wily fox who has outwitted a score of packs and killed a dozen times meets a mercifully quick death in a bite from the leading hound.

The friendly, sure-footed hounds of the mountain packs are not the only hounds out on the Lakeland fells during these short winter days. Towards the end of January you will see their first cousins, the faster, slimmer trail-hounds, below the snow line practising for the coming season. A slow job, demanding much patience, this training of a trail-hound. When the puppy is seven or eight months old and has begun to hunt "scents" in the lanes around the farm it is time to try it across a couple of fields, following the trail of an old stocking dipped in aniseed and paraffin. At first the little fellow is more interested in the piece of meat he has seen the trailer take out of his pocket, but in time, after months of patient work, he will follow the trail for its own sake. Perhaps it's only a funny game at first, but when he is an old dog he will be ready to chase the sharp scent for ten miles across the most mountainous country in England, without stopping to drink even on the hottest day. And while the puppies are frisking about near the farm their elders, fat and sleepy after months of idleness and good food, are getting their weight down in practice higher up in the fells. And there are two more months of this before the season starts.

2

WINTER WEATHER
February

FROM the top of the fell behind my house I could see half the Lake District—the Coniston Fells, Bowfell and the Langdales, with the Scafells peeping up behind, Fairfield, Red Screes, the Kentmere hills, the climb over Shap summit, the Howgills, and the nearer foothills. All were plastered in snow, gleaming white in the dazzling sunshine pouring down out of a cloudless blue sky. Except for the brown trees in the snow-capped wood and the grass in the lee of the grey stone walls, there were no other colours—just a great white hummocky world beneath a Mediterranean sky.

The change from the previous day, with its hours of continuous snow, its leaden skies, and its wretched visibility, could hardly have been more remarkable. Overnight we had been transported from the Antarctic of our imagination to the paradise of the winter sports posters. A handful of sheep nosed among the patchy snow at the edge of the wood, a tiny shrew or mountain mouse crept out of a hollow and scurried across the snow, and Sambo floundered in and out of the deep drifts, his head plastered in white from constant burrowing. Not another living thing in sight and not a sound. I pointed my ski-tips towards the roof-tops away below and slid silently down for the six o'clock news. In another hour the quiet deserted fell-side would be alive with a hundred youngsters, released from school and tea, with their toboggans, tea trays, and dogs;

laughing, yelling and barking until long after the stars had come out.

That was the February of 1960 but, down the years, there have been many other different February days—wild, wet days, days of storm and flood, and calm, sunny days. Let me try to recall some of them.

One day, trudging quietly in the new snow, up through the Wythburn woods to the Helvellyn ridge, I edged round a shoulder of fell and suddenly found myself staring hard at a fine red deer only a few yards away. Before I could put down my load and reach for a camera he had time to give me a hard, disdainful look and throw up his head, silhouetted against the snow, in "Monarch of the Glen" defiance. Then, his dainty heels kicking up a flurry of snow, he had disappeared. Another day we came upon a fine stag picking his way down the Longsleddale side of Gatescarth Pass. He had not seen us and I was creeping into camera range when a tinkling pebble made him swing round. A glance of sudden fear and then, without even a crouch to spring, he was over the wall in one lovely bound and trotting nimbly down the valley through the snow patches. For five minutes we watched him, a fugitive from something he did not understand, as he jogged down towards the intake fields, leaving us trespassers in his domain. The snows had driven him down from the heights and he would have a long detour, over the Mosedale fells down to Haweswater, and up through the crags to get back to his own country in Riggindale or Ramsgill.

Unless you go deliberately searching for red deer in their homes in the lonely upland corries of Martindale and Bannerdale or the Helvellyn woods you rarely stumble upon them on the fells. They are very shy, and unless the wind is in your favour they will know of your approach from more than a mile away. The snow had sent these animals—with probably others of their herds—on food-foraging expeditions. The red deer are by no means disappearing from Lakeland, and they are certainly widening their territories. From Martindale, their sanctuary since medieval days, they have crossed Ullswater to the Helvellyn mountains, wandered far south into the Furness home of the roe deer, and even reached the central Cumberland range.

These unexpected encounters with wild creatures, especially

in the winter months when the fells are little visited, are wonderfully rewarding. Another February day, in the hills above
Threshthwaite Cove, east of Kirkstone, we saw a sleepy fox,
sunning himself on the screes. He didn't notice us until we gave
him a shout, and even then didn't seem greatly worried. He
watched us for a second or two, decided we were too far off to
be dangerous, and then trotted slowly up the screes and across
the snowdrifts to the top of Thornthwaite Crag. Now and again
he stopped, looked round disdainfully, and then ambled on,
zigzagging up the steep slope with his long brush dragging
behind him. Tomorrow, I thought, he may be running for his
life from the yelping hounds and he may be after the young
lambs in the valley in a week or two, but that day he was just
taking a stroll, with effortless ease, across his homeland fells.

An hour later we surprised three red deer that had climbed
to the summit track across the High Street the Romans used,
and had halted to sniff the wind. For a moment they stood in
the sunlight on the ridge, a statuesque group of lovely, dainty
animals, and then one of them spotted us. He whispered to the
others, and in a flash they bounded noiselessly away, over the
edge and down to the tarn. There was a little knot of Fell
ponies a few hundred yards further on, quietly grazing just
below the 2,5000-feet contour line and quite unconcerned by our
approach. Like the red fox and the red deer these wild, shaggy
creatures with their fine, black manes hanging over the eyes, their
tufted coats, and their long, thick tails, were happily at home in
their own hills, and we left them undisturbed.

The pine marten, they say, is around and about again on the
fells. Some years ago he was thought to be extinct, but now and
again one hears tales of huntsmen seeing a flurry of brown
scurrying along an old stone wall, or the flash of his whitish
chest as he wriggles down a hole. You don't go out to look for a
pine marten in the Lake District, but rather consider yourself
lucky if you catch a glimpse of something that might be him. He
must be the shyest of animals and there may be only a few
handfuls of them hanging on to a precarious existence—probably in the comparative safety of the forestry plantations. If
hounds run one into a bield they seem to make even more fuss
than if they had holed a fox. Perhaps the smell annoys them.
This is understandable for the pine marten is only called the

'sweet mart' because he is not quite so objectionable as his cousin, the polecat. Sixty or seventy years ago pine martens were fairly common in the higher fells. I've not heard of the polecat being seen, but then he was more a creature of the marsh lands and peat bogs. Many years ago they would be common enough, along with the wild cat, but those days, and the still earlier ones of the wild boar, are long passed. Strange, therefore, that the badger, once extinct, should be with us again, and now the pine marten.

A skein of eight greylag geese in arrowhead formation, long necks extended, went honking across the evening sky over Winster on their way to the estuary. How many, I wondered, would return? For the wintry weather is indirectly taking its toll of these fine birds. Normally they are winter visitors or passage-migrants in the fell country, but some time ago a scheme was started to introduce them in a wild state to the area in the hope that they might be persuaded to become a nesting species. The newcomers were brought from the north-west Highlands and encouraged to nest on small islands in the middle of tarns sited not far from the coast. Here they were safe from the foxes—until the ice came. But by February the foxes were crossing the frozen meres and seeking out the plump grey-brown geese, and so the greylags, not unnaturally, decided to roost elsewhere, preferably on the estuary. Every evening, once the frost tightened on the ponds, they have been flying out over the woods and across the sands, but many of them, on the way out or on their return to the islands have been falling prey to marksmen lying in wait near the coast. And so the wildfowlers who themselves introduced the geese to the area had to appeal to their fellows to stay their hand and allow the greylags to settle in. A few years ago a national count of grey geese discovered none in the area, although hundreds may pass through in the autumn and winter. It would be a pity if the wildfowlers' enterprise is to be ruined by this thoughtless killing.

The sheep "trods" that encircle and criss-cross the fells have always fascinated me. How old are the oldest of them? Why do they go this way or that? Presumably fell sheep are never lost, even in the thickest mist. You might disturb three or four Herdwicks sheltering in the lee of a rocky summit, as I've often

done, and they'll scatter in all directions, vanishing immediately if there's mist about. No doubt the sheep know their
tiny "trods" as well as we know the roads around our homes,
but it's not often that these miniature footpaths are of any use
to the traveller in the hills. They have a habit of contouring
without making or losing height and they inevitably lead nowhere—nowhere, that is, to a human being. Yet some of them
might have been in use for hundreds of years. Under snow they
are, of course, invisible, but the sheep still take the same
routes and seem to know where they are going. One day, when
I've the time and energy, I must try and produce a map of all
the sheep "trods" on a single Lakeland mountain—a criss-cross
of ancient and sensible rights of way, contouring the fells with
careful deliberation and crossing the becks at just the right
places—for sheep. It could be a revealing task.

At this time of the year you're never very far away from the
merry sounds of tree felling and hedge laying—the solid crunch
of the woodman's axe, the staccato chopping of the hedger's
lighter weapon, and, now and again, the slow crashing through
the matted undergrowth of some fine old-timer with the final
expressive thud at the end. Everywhere, it seems, up and down
the dales men are busy chopping down trees, and one wonders,
with some alarm, whether planting is going on at the same
rate. In the large woodlands these matters are taken care of
nowadays by the Forestry Commission, and elsewhere the local
authorities have responsibility, but all this by no means pre-
cludes indiscriminate felling. Here in Westmorland it is estimated we are losing two thousand hedgerow trees—oak, ash,
birch, larch, and many others—every year, and, more often than
not, the young saplings are being slaughtered too. Hedges are
being laid clean nowadays instead of a young tree left every few
yards. Some farmers hardly seem to be concerned nowadays
to provide shelter for the grazing cattle of future generations,
and road widening takes its toll of many fine trees. So that
gradually in places the appearance of the countryside is changing. But although felling can leave ugly patches in once lovely
coppices there is one compensation—the glorious wild wealth
of foxgloves, bluebells, primroses, willow herb, and the shy
wood anemone that often follows.

Trimming slates at Spout Crag Quarry, Elterwater

One recent February they finished thinning the tangled wood over the hill at the foot of the scar behind my house, and a small corner of the Lake District was transformed. Where there used to be just a dark square of dense matted undergrowth against the fellside and a thousand trees fighting for the light became a trim woodland of birch and ash—straight slender trunks in white and brown soon to be clothed in their first shimmer of green. You could hardly struggle through the wood before for, besides the twisted, thorny brushwood, there was the additional hazard of great blocks of limestone lying concealed in the dank undergrowth. This craziest of crazy paving has been dropping down from the scar for a thousand years or more, but now it has all been dragged out and sold for rockeries—without the slightest detriment to anybody or the scene. And soon the once dark woodland became a wonderland of primroses, blue-bells, foxgloves, wood anemones, and many other shy flowers. Once again after a lapse of generations, it became a delight to walk through the wood along its rich, new carpet, with the sky now showing overhead and the sunlight slanting through the trees. I remember they marked the trees for keeping with dabs of blue paint, and the tractors and the saws dealt with the others, while great fires consumed the brushwood.

One of the fanciful attractions of the townsman for the country is the smell of woodsmoke. The memory of a few fragrant whiffs inhaled when he drops down to the farms in the valley after a winter's day in the fells is enough to make the man, looking out over crowded rooftops, sigh for lost days in the open air among friendly dalesfolk. The scent of woodsmoke for him can be as nostalgic as the sight of his tattered rucksack and boots, an old map, or faded photographs of carefree hours. I live in the country, two miles out towards the hills from Kendal, but burn logs on my drawing-room fire basically for economic reasons. In theory it sounds all right. Whenever you see a dead branch you put it in the back of the car and then cut it up on an electric saw. But in practice it never works out that way. You either have to grow trees and cut them down or buy them in loads of logs. I once bought a tree, or rather its branches —the owner had the trunk—for £5 and it lasted me all winter, but the logs were far too big to go on the fire and had to be split with immense labour. Nowadays I get a load from the

3

Ill Bell from St. Raven's Edge
February snows: Froswick with Ill Bell

farmer at about the same cost but there's still a lot of axing to be done, as well as carting and stacking, and each night the fire consumes a wheelbarrow full of logs. My latest pile is the remains of a big dead ash that I persuaded the farmer needed felling, but the heap is dwindling rapidly. It smells wonderful from the garden—if you care to venture out on a winter's night —but you don't notice it much inside. But now I'm growing my own firewood, although it will be ten years at least before the trees are ready for thinning.

For more than three hundred years Lake District men with names like Rigg, Bland, Grisedale, and Tyson had been winning Westmorland green slate from an enormous crater hidden among the foothills of Wetherlam, until a generation or so ago when they decided the quarry was worked out. But in recent years the old workings have sprung into life again, and, if you climb steeply through the larches and the silver birch, guided by the shrill whirr of the diamond cutter, you will find the young adventurers in their pleasant eyrie—sturdy remnants of a dwindling band of rural craftsmen. Rather a piratical, devil-may-care crew they seemed when first I called a few years ago— one with a great red beard, another with a wooden leg, and a third with one quizzical eye. But with what precision and dexterity they rived the lovely sea-green slate, the best, they say, in England! There are only half a dozen places in the Lake District where you will find slate of just this colour, but more than one old roof speaks of its resistance to two hundred years of rain and frost. You reach the floor of the quarry through a tunnel three hundred yards long laboriously hacked out by hand through the solid rock. The walls of the quarry tower vertically for three hundred feet and high above your head you can see where the first tunnel of the seventeenth-century pioneers came through. You'll never see a bigger man-made hole in this part of the world.

Most "Westmorland" green slate is quarried in the Lancashire and Cumberland parts of Lakeland nowadays but it is satisfying to notice that this almost everlasting product of the fells is becoming known in many distant parts of the world. Everybody has heard that Westmorland green slates are the best in the country, but now architects and builders are demanding huge blocks of this splendid rock as facing stone for important new buildings in places as remote as Melbourne, Calcutta, and Cape Town. Old quarries, abandoned years ago are being opened up again to cope with the new demand, but skilled labour is difficult to get. Youngsters in the dales don't go in for quarrying nowadays, as their fathers and grandfathers did. They go for jobs in the towns, and a fine local industry with long traditions risks being slowly strangled just when its biggest chances lie ahead. In years to come the daleman's skill of knowing good rock and how to work it could be lost forever—despite bigger pay packets—in the same way that the ancient craft of dry-stone walling disappeared from the valleys until the recent revival of interest. There is a fine, adventurous spirit behind some of these new quarrying enterprises and several of the quarries themselves are really exciting places—tremendous holes where you could hide a cathedral.

February days of exciting colour in Lakeland—gleaming snows, skies of poster blue, the surprising reds, browns and greys of the rocks in new relief, the magical, golden sunsets—are sometimes followed by wild nights of almost Arctic severity on the high passes. On the main highway into Scotland, 1,400 feet up on the bleak Shap Fells, snow is often lying in drifts several feet deep, and the road itself, darkly zigzagging through a silent, white world, as slippery, at times, as an ice-rink. The tough long-distance lorry men who traverse this road several times a week are not particularly worried about these conditions, but when they are met on the summit by blinding blizzards and cannot distinguish the road ahead from the terrible drop over the edge they have to stop and ride out the storm somehow. Sometimes the drivers have sat huddled in their draughty cabs waiting for the dawn; other men have left their lorries half buried in the drifts and staggered, knee or waist deep in the snow, down the steep, twisting miles to the bright lights of the Jungle Café, which every lorry driver knows. And all through these long, wild nights roadmen, called out from warm homes, have been working bravely, blue with cold, their gloved hands freezing to their spades, to keep the great road, main artery of Westmorland and the North, open at all costs.

Up there in the biting cold it is often hard to tell whether it's snowing or not, for on many February nights the wind comes scourging out of the north-east, whipping the snow off the fells in a blinding fury and swirling it into the roads. So that as fast as one bit of road is cleared it is all blown over again, and the roadmen are denied even the satisfaction of a job well done. These are the real heroes of the storm—these and the road scouts—and the lorry-drivers, regretfully, are sometimes the villains. Their tradition, to get through at all costs, sounds noble enough but too often the clumsy articulated vehicles prove unable to cope with the snow and ice, and the road may be blocked for hours to traffic which otherwise could have got through. But soon the new motorway through the Lune valley should avoid the worst perils of winter by taking a more sheltered route at an easier gradient, although the passage of these last fells before the Border will always have its problems in the worst of the blizzards.

February is often an excellent month for ski-ing in the fells, and one of the more popular areas is on the north-east slopes of Raise, near Helvellyn. You set off hopefully for the ski-ing slopes by driving up the steep winding road from the lake towards the former lead mines, and we used to leave the car at the top of the last hairpin—if we could get that far. Nowadays, there may be restrictions. The height is about 1,000 feet above sea level and you are on a level with the great banks of spoil which used to look so ugly from the top of Helvellyn, two miles away and 2,000 feet higher. But coarse sea grasses have now been sown on the unnatural slopes, and most of the mine buildings that in winter made the place look something like a shanty town in the wilds of Alaska, have been pulled down. But you are still 1,000 feet or more below the ski-ing slopes, and the zigzags up the fellside have to be climbed with the awkward load of skis and sticks on your shoulder. The higher you trudge the better the views below and to the east, and soon you can look across to the Pennines beyond the Eden valley. Some distance below the summit of the range that separates Cumberland and Westmorland you reach your destination—a long, steep drift of snow facing north-east which, in an exceptional year, has provided ski-ing in May. Perhaps it was raining when you left the valley and a most unlikely day for the job, but here you are in a different world—a world, if you are lucky, of crisp snow, blue skies, and sharp, distant views. The only slightly foreign note is struck by the throbbing engine of the ski-tow, a workmanlike piece of machinery and a great boon when it is working, but an unusual object on a mountain top.

Often there are less pleasant days on Raise. I remember one February day in 1962 with driving rain sweeping across the fells and a gale making even motoring difficult, while on the tops conditions were nearly as bad as you can get in this country. At about 1,000 feet the torrential rain turned to sleet and hail and 500 feet higher a snow blizzard was raging through the hills, so that in minutes we were plastered white and our cheeks battered red and raw with the onslaught. The game was more like Antarctic exploration than the gay winter sports of the holiday posters and I suppose we wondered what on earth we were doing up there instead of keeping warm and cosy in the valley. On top of our chosen slope of steep snow blown into ice lay several inches of new snow and every now and again this would be swept along the contours by a sudden, fierce gust almost blinding us in its fury. Half the time we could neither see where we were nor, occasionally, even hear ourselves speak. It was also difficult to remain upright and very, very cold. But we survived and back in the valley, wet through and a little battered, it was curious to notice that the fells, seen from south to west, showed no signs of snow and looked merely wet. All the snow had been blown on to the north and east slopes where it must have been lying, in places, up to ten feet deep. At last we could enjoy it all in retrospect —a hot bath, and the pleasant thought of warm, dry clothes, food and drink. And then, suddenly, it all seems worth while.

But sometimes winter mountain days turn out much better than expected. One February day in 1963 when most of the north of England was shrouded in fog four of us had the good fortune to enjoy two or three hours of warm sunshine, crisp snow, and perfect visibility. From the lanes at the foot of the fells north of Appleby, their red sandstone walls almost aflame in the morning sun, there seemed no possibility of ski-ing on the tops—no more than a few scattered patches of snow—but these things can be deceptive. Feeling slightly ashamed of ourselves, for mountains should be climbed on foot, we motored up the former mine road—the highest in England—and found, on the north-east slopes of Great Dun Fell, snowdrifts a quarter of a mile long, hard as a board and irresistible. It seemed almost too good to be true—not a breath of wind on a summit where we nearly always meet biting gales, perfect snow less than five minutes' walk from the car, sunshine, magnificent views and the whole mountain to ourselves. We lunched in the tumble-down ruins of a lonely bothy probably built for the miners a hundred, two hundred years ago, for nobody else came this way, and nobody goes there now except walkers and skiers. Perhaps there is no lonelier expanse of moorland in the country. The late afternoon sun warmed the fellsides so that they glowed yellow and orange, and, but for the frozen snow at our feet, it might have been early autumn. Easily, we motored homewards through the crisp starlight and then, four miles from streets and houses, met the fog.

Another February day after a week of drizzle and rain with the hills hidden in mist we were clambering, wet through and rather miserable, up the dark, steep corridors of Rossett Gill in Langdale. Visibility was only a few yards and I remember we thought it rather cheering to come across the tracks of a fox in the snow, and then, all at once, we saw we were climbing into a completely new world. As we trudged out of the dark gully and up to the Westmorland county boundary we saw the swirl-ing mists sink slowly beneath us, and the snow-covered tops of the fells, magnified into Alpine giants, rise majestically out of the shadows into the morning sunlight. What a thrill to step out of the sodden darkness on to the crisp, white plateau with its backcloth of shining, distant peaks!—the sort of thrill the shepherd or mountaineer captures only occasionally, and the rest of the world never. After that, even the dry sandwiches tasted good, and it was hard to realize that down below it was "just another clarty Lakeland day".

Whenever there's heavy snow in Westmorland these days we think of that desperate winter nearly twenty years ago. Conditions today are sometimes described as "nearly as bad as", or perhaps "nothing like" 1947—never worse. I remember they even had to keep postponing the budget meeting of the county council and the youngsters' scholarship examinations because both councillors and school-children were more or less marooned in their villages. A train disappeared in a snowdrift and at one time the telegraph poles near the summit of the Shap Fells road were only just poking out of the snow. People were happily ski-ing in the high, north-facing drifts as late as May, but hundreds of sheep were lost and some farmers were years recovering from the disaster.

The wild weather must be terribly trying for dumb creatures. One day in the Mallerstang area we came upon a lorry load of cows stuck in the middle of an eight-foot drift miles from any-where in a bitter north-east wind. They had been up on that bleak moorland two days and two nights, and every so often a cowman had to squeeze into the box, milk his charges, and later give then some milk to drink. There was no other food. Another day near Patterdale we found perhaps a dozen sheep huddled in the lee side of a fell wall, and slowly being covered by the blown snow. They preferred being buried with snow in comparative shelter to foraging beneath the shallower snow in the freezing wind. The mass of closely wedged fleeces did not stir but we knew they were alive. In an hour or so they would be completely covered over, but the prospect did not occasion panic. They seemed to be awaiting their fate with unblinking fortitude, glad for the moment of the warmth from the others. We told the farmer about them on the way down, but both he and I have known sheep being buried for a fortnight and still alive. On the frozen road a rabbit had just been crushed by a motor-car and already the crows, as hungry as all other wild creatures in the new white wilderness, were at work on it. And these are the days when the foxes come down to the farms to look for poultry, for there must be little food about when the countryside is transformed into a white wilderness.

Later when the becks are in glorious spate and the fellsides sodden with the melted snows, is the time to go out and look at waterfalls. None of our dozen or so notable falls are very large compared, for instance, with the biggest in Scotland, and when seen by the summer crowds appear, as often as not, little better than rather dreary trickles. What on earth, we have sometimes wondered, was Robert Southey getting so excited about when he described, in several hundred brilliantly chosen words, exactly how the water comes down at Lodore? But a visit to any one of these cataracts at just the right time in February or March, with the crowds gone and only a few browsing Herdwicks for company will make it all perfectly clear. One February day I chose Aira Force, near Ullswater. The traffic was rolling past on the main road five minutes' walk away but nobody else had bothered to stroll up to the fall. A pity, for the scene was quite breathtaking. The whole gorge seemed alive with the thunder of the force and its clouds of rising spray, and I've no doubt that every few seconds thousands of tons of churning water were crashing and pounding down the rocks. From afar off I had heard the roar of the fall and then, suddenly, as I came through the dripping trees, there it was straight ahead—Nature in her most savage mood, angry, merciless and menacing, and irresistible. In their agony, the brown surging waters seemed to writhe and scream in their sickening plunge. The Poet Laureate, I thought, had been right after all.

3

CREATURES OF THE WILD
March

THE daffodils were fighting their way through the snow drifts
at the bottom of my garden, and the forsythia and gooseberry
bushes budding nicely, but these seemed the only signs of
spring in the wintry world of March 1962. All the main roads
had been cleared of snow, but you could still get stuck in drifts
on some of the minor roads and on several of the lanes leading
to the remoter farms. A waterfall by the side of Kirkstone Pass
had quite disappeared—first frozen over and then buried in a
hanging drift—and all the becks were stilled. I passed some
sheep, perhaps fifty of them, just brought down from the tops
and feeding ravenously on piles of baled hay, but the birds,
apart from the ravens, seemed to have been blown out of the
sky. Except for the wind, whistling distantly through the
crags, the countryside was strangely quiet and still—waiting,
some dalesfolk said, for worse blizzards to come. But the mountains were not nearly so plastered with snow as one might have
expected. Fierce north-easterlies had blown it off the fells and
into the roads and the flatter intake fields so that in places it was
easier to trudge up through the bracken and the ling than along
the tarmac. The northern and eastern slopes were merely dusted
with snow over the old drifts, but you could be up to your waist
on the slopes facing the setting sun within ten yards of your car.
And the evening sky looked savage—a fiery orange flecked with
angry black and grey. The winter seemed far from over.

Another March two tiny patches of snow still hanging just

below the broad summit of High Street were the only reminders in the view from my window that winter might not yet be over, but elsewhere spring was on the way. The grass was beginning to green over again, there were shy splashes of blue and yellow beneath the hedges, the village gardens filled with flowering bulbs, and the birches ready to burst into leaf. In the dales the first few lambs had already arrived, but it would be some weeks before the fell sheep dropped their young. It should be a good crop, I thought, and most farmers expected an average of three lambs from every two sheep. On the fells the ewes had still to be coaxed down from their "heaf" to unfamiliar but safer ground nearer the homestead, and from the top of our rock climb in Combe Gill above Borrowdale one March day we could see dozens of mothers-to-be sedately picking their way across the screes. In a week or two it should be possible to walk for miles across the high fells and not see a single sheep. It was sunny enough to sit perched on the summit rocks all the afternoon without feeling chilled. Until a giant plane came droning over the fells the only sounds for an hour had been an occasional slither of scree, the tinkle of pails whispered up the fell from the farm below, and the monotonous drip, drip of wet moss in the gully. The sun peeping over the mountain wall at the head of the dale shone on the ploughing, liming, and manuring in a dozen distant fields, and spring seemed nearer still.

March days of biting winds from the north are anxious days for the sheep farmer, although it is the end of April before the Herdwicks from the higher fells begin lambing. One Westmorland farmer friend of mine looks after the birth of something like two thousand lambs every March—a big job for any man. I don't suppose he could ever tell you the exact size of his flock, but he told me one March he had about 2,200 lambing ewes, perhaps 700 gimmers and hoggs—females and males, between one and two years old—and around 300 wethers or castrated rams. This meant that with any luck at all he would have perhaps 5,000 sheep by May—one of the biggest flocks in the north. I well remember the early months of 1947 when we had the heaviest snows that have reached Westmorland this century. This was the winter when a train was buried near Barras station in North Westmorland and they had to call out troops to clear the cuttings. In places on the way to Penrith the telegraph lines were only just peeping above the great banks of snow, and one morning a man passed my house on skis—on his way to his office in Kendal.

It was a terrible winter for the farmers and the sheep losses were appalling. One estimate was that two million sheep were lost in the whole country and certainly many thousands were lost in and around Lakeland. In Westmorland it was estimated that about forty per cent of the breeding ewes died, and the lamb crop was the smallest for many years. The two lonely Birkdale farms in the north-east corner of the county lost nearly all their sheep—about 110 survivors with thirty lambs out of one flock of about seven hundred, and only forty-five sheep and seven lambs out of the other similarly sized flock.

Some remarkable performances were put up by the sheep-dogs at this time. One fourteen-years-old dog called Hemp owned by the farmer at Bull Pot, a high, remote farm near Kirkby Lonsdale, is said to have rescued more than one hundred sheep from snow drifts, "setting" them for the shepherd to dig out. One of these sheep had been buried under four feet of snow for six or seven weeks but was still alive when rescued.

The early months of 1951 also brought a great deal of snow and by March of that year it was reported that some villages in north Westmorland had had nearly fifty snowfalls already that winter. That March skiers were enjoying the best Lake District winter many of them could remember, and in the north-facing gullies climbers were out each week-end hacking steps up the steep ice pitches and burrowing through the great overhanging cornices of snow into the winter sunshine at the top.

And hidden under the frozen snow many a mountain ewe, missed when the sheep were brought down to the lower fields, would be lying dead, while others, far away from visible food, might be starving. But not all the sheep tragedies would be from hunger, for many meet their deaths on the crags. They creep down the upper ledges of the precipices seeking out the more succulent grasses and herbs, and then find they can't get up the crag again. A few are rescued but some, weak with hunger after being marooned for days or weeks on the cliffs, fall over the edge as they try to escape to easier ground. And, perhaps weeks later, after the ravens have done their gruesome work the shepherd, combing the gullies, finds the pitiful remains.

There's an old Lakeland theory that the best way to deal
with a cragfast sheep is to leave her on the crag until she wastes
away into a bundle of wool. You then simply push her over the
edge and she will float safely down to earth. We thought rather
enviously of this simple, if slightly inhumane, method on
a March day in 1955 when we were wrestling with two sheep
above a hundred-feet overhang on Whitbarrow Scar. The
farmers said they had been up there three weeks but, judging by
their strength, determination and agility, we thought it would
be many more weeks before they were ready for the parachute
method. They seemed perfectly content, snatching at the odd
tuft of grass wedged in a crevice, until we got near enough with
the rope. Their only thought then was to leap over the edge—if
possible dragging us with them. We might get a loop round
one of their necks and have high hopes—while almost swinging
in mid-air—of getting the forelegs in as well; then suddenly she
would be out of the noose and slithering over the edge, with her
former foothold crashing on to the screes below. There were
moments when one's own lifeline looked woefully thin. I don't
know what we'd have done if the sheep had been of the hornless
variety. As it was, we discovered that a pair of horns makes an
excellent belaying pin and that once you could lash one of them
to a convenient root you could begin to think out the next move.
These two fought hard all through their hour-long rescue even
when, as often happened, they were hanging upside down. And,
once safe on the screes, with comfortable grazing close at hand,
they still glared at us and seemed to look longingly at their
remote ledge.

I remember, too, another sheep-rescuing adventure on Rains-
barrow Crag in Kentmere where a ewe and two lambs had been
marooned for some time. The lambs were dealt with fairly
easily, but the old ewe proved much more recalcitrant. She was
on a ledge, about one yard wide, from which all the grass had
been consumed and the problem was the usual one of how to get
close enough to grab her before she panicked and leapt over the
edge. I was secure on a rope well held from above and I had
another rope with a sling on the end in which I planned to tie
the sheep. The drop below was noticeable, if not considerable,
but the men holding my rope knew what they were about. In
the end the job was done with a little elementary guile. I edged

along the ledge holding in my hand a bait of tasty grass which
the ewe could hardly resist, and then managed to grab her with
a sort of rugger tackle as she tried to spring. There was a
second or two of rather undignified heaving and scrabbling
before she was trussed up and could be hauled up the crag to a
safe place and then lowered in easy stages to the screes.

Sometimes you come upon a fox shoot on the fells in March.
In some counties it is said to be a terrible thing to shoot a fox,
but in Westmorland it is just another method of keeping them
down. Gunmen may not be particularly popular with the hunting dalesfolk, but there seems to be plenty of scope for both of
them. There must have been twenty guns spread out along
the shoulder of Harter Fell above Mardale one sunny March
Sunday, besides the beaters who made enough noise to scare
everything off the fells for weeks. Four fine vixen were quickly
killed seconds after they had darted out across the snow, and a
day or two later were in some London laboratory, for Ministry
officials were investigating their eating habits about that time.
The Ministry were then paying 7s. 6d. for each dead fox and
helping out with the cartridges—they may pay more now—but
as this was an organized shoot the money would be ploughed
back into the funds of the local pest destruction society. Members bagging a fox on their own—perhaps a farmer defending
his new lambs—would reap the benefit for they would get the
7s. 6d. doubled by the society. The gunmen had expected more
foxes this time—the sort of mild windless day when Reynard
loves to lie out in the sun—but it was generally agreed that
four vixen was a fair bag. Only the terriers, who would have
been happier hunting, looked a trifle disappointed.

Another day in Longsleddale I saw that the shooters had
accounted for three foxes. Scent had been lying badly on the
parched fellside for some time and many of the foxes put up by
the hounds had managed to escape. The lambs born lower down
the dale that week would now be safer and the fell farmer would
certainly be happier about his Swaledales due to lamb on April
10th. Although the gunmen have only a poor opinion of the
hunters, who in turn probably think even less of the marksmen,
the farmer was right when he told me; "When they've both
done, there's still a terrible lot of foxes about." Those cunning

freebooters of the fells, the bird-nesters, were also about that day in the morning sunshine, secretly combing the crags for ravens' eggs, and hoping, perhaps, to locate the elusive peregrine. We had seen the ravens earlier, a fine pair performing lively acrobatics over the crag, but, although probably watching from some eyrie, they were nowhere to be seen when the robbers arrived, It would be justice, we thought, if the gunmen could frighten away the egg-thieves who have been a real menace for many years.

One March day I watched a lone fell hound, two hours behind the hunt and so weary he could hardly lift one leg in front of another, crawl down the steep side of Nab Scar above Rydal after a hard day on the tops and steer unerringly for the farmhouse where he had been fed the previous night. As he sank down on the straw in the barn I saw he had a nasty badger wound on his jaw. The badger, no friend of the Lakeland fox-hunter, has been on the increase in recent years among the woods that skirt the high fells, and several have been killed, but before meeting their end they have often badly punished both hounds and terriers. Another day two game little terriers had a terrible battle with a most determined old badger, and then limped uncomplainingly down to the valley with pieces torn out of noses and feet. Without a whimper they submitted to treatment by the red-coated huntsman—Anthony Chapman of the Coniston pack—which must have made the nasty open wounds sting painfully. They would, I knew, be out of action some time. It is mostly after dusk on summer nights when the badger comes out of his hiding in the woods but he is much too careful to be more than very rarely seen. A few years ago I remember one creeping out on to the Windermere–Newby Bridge road and being suddenly illuminated, drinking in a pool, by the headlights of my car.

Up near the top of Kirkstone Pass one damp March morning the mist, swirling in grey, boiling clouds over the crumbling stone walls, was so thick that although there had been some watery sunshine five minutes earlier down in the valley I had to switch on my sidelights. A moment later I nearly ran into a man leading a trail hound, and then, a few yards from the summit, straggling along the side of the winding wall, there were perhaps a score of men in caps and breeches, each with his hound on a short lead. Our hound-trailing season had not yet begun, but this was a practice trail, and the trailer with his odorous bag was due in from his long tramp over the fells in a few minutes. While we watched, the men got their hounds into line, took off their leads, and waited, one knee on the damp ground, for the start. Long before the trailer appeared like a Brocken Spectre out of the mist you could tell from the excitement of the hounds that he was approaching. Then, suddenly, there he was, rather further to the left than we had expected. There was a sharp whistle in place of the dropped handkerchief and, with a chorus of delighted yelps, the hounds were away, leaping in a mad jumble of muzzles and legs into the swirling whiteness. There was nothing to see, so the men sat down to wait. But soon the hounds would be back, hearts thumping and coats glistening with moisture after their five to six miles run over the roughest ground in England.

On my way up Raise for the ski-ing one Sunday morning in March I watched at least a score of red deer bounding down over the snow patches, or quietly searching for mosses among the boulders—the biggest herd I had seen on the fells for years. They say the red deer population of Lakeland is more than holding its own in the eastern fells, due mostly to careful preservation in the Martindale area, but elsewhere there is much senseless persecution of red, roe, and fallow deer. One even hears stories from time to time of well-equipped expeditions from the towns carrying out wholesale slaughter—quite apart from local poaching—and in a few places the graceful creatures have been almost exterminated.

It was, I think, a sensible decision to exercise some measure of control over these elegant creatures, the last big game in England. The farmers and landowners who have been grumbling about the damage they have been doing should be satisfied, while the best of the animals will be preserved as an important Lakeland asset. When they are hungry, which is often enough in winter, these shy, graceful beasts can be a menace in the valleys. They come down off the snow-covered fells, strip the bark from the young trees, gobble off the tops of the new conifers, and eat practically everything within sight. They seem particularly fond of turnips, cabbages, potatoes, wheat and oats, and half a dozen of them can ruin an acre's crop in no time. But, on the other hand, the red deer is part of the Lakeland scene and has been for hundreds of years, and it would be a thousand pities if he was to be exterminated. He is still without legal status or protection and can be shot at will at all seasons in England, provided one has a game licence and the permission of the land-owner—and also provided it is not a Sunday or Christmas Day. Some of us think this is all wrong. We protect scores of varieties of birds but deer, the largest and the most beautiful of our game and creatures of unique interest, seem to have no protection whatever. Now that they are to be preserved, cannot they also be protected.

The former game warden to the Forestry Commission (Mr. H. A. Fooks) used to live in the middle of the Grisedale forest in a cottage filled with heads of deer, the skins of leopard and tiger, and such assorted articles as crocodile's feet, books on birds, and German beer mugs. In place of ivy on the outer walls there were several fine pairs of stags' antlers, and the little garden was filled with the song of canaries and shamas, keeping company with a few dozen pheasants, Polish bantams, and even stranger looking birds. Mr. Fooks, a large, much-travelled man, loves all animals, birds, and flowers, and even confesses to an affection for reptiles, but his job in those days was to keep down the deer population in these parts to reasonable limits. He had to get rid of the actual animals causing the damage, thin out the old and the feeble, and build up as many fine, healthy, well-fed specimens as the area could comfortably hold. You would see him going off with his rifle one afternoon to stalk some troublesome old stag and the next morning scouring the countryside for sphagnum moss to enrich the diet of his other charges during the coming winter months. And the important work, a job for experts only, still goes on.

Some of the days in March 1956, particularly the mornings, were incredibly lovely in the southern Lake District, and only a slight haze over the fells prevented perfection. Perhaps some people may think the view of the Langdale Pikes from Low-wood rather hackneyed, but one morning I remember it seemed freshly beautiful. The lake, rippled by a strong north breeze, was the richest blue, the familiar outline of the fells, with the rain-washed crags glinting in the morning sunlight looked bold

The Kirkstone road: bringing down the sheep
Ice floes on Red Tarn with Striding Edge

and inviting, a gateway to the higher glories of the inner sanctuary, while the silvery shores under the birch trees and the warm colours in the old stone walls completed the foreground. Behind, the fells presented the perfect backcloth—blue skies with billowing white clouds so magnificently grouped that a painter or colour photographer would have chosen a low horizon and allowed the clouds to make the picture. The more one studies the Lake District "out of season" the more one is convinced that holiday-makers who know it only in July or August see it at its worst—washed-out colours, poor distant views, dust and enervating heat or incessant rain, crowded roads, and coaches by the score. In almost any other season you can hope for better weather, better views, more peace and quiet, and a natural countryside rather than a trippers' paradise.

When March 1963 came smilingly in I thought that for the healthy lover of the open air there would never be a finer winter in the Lake District than this one had been. There hadn't been a drop of rain in Langdale—often one of the wettest places in England—for seventy days, there were long hours of sunshine in February and March and the mountains were covered in crisp, unbroken snow. It must have been a long, hard winter for the old and the ailing, but the young and the fit will remember the early months of 1963 in the fell country with gratitude. For weeks there had been ski-ing, skating, snow-climbing, and invigorating mountain walking in almost every corner of the fells, under the sort of conditions usually found only in the Alpine countries. I could ski in the field at the back of my house or skate on the pond just over the hill, although there happened to be better places further afield. Indeed, we seemed to be getting spoiled for choice, and some of us were perhaps beginning to take for granted those days of cloudless, blue skies; I couldn't remember when I had last worn a raincoat. The sun awakened me in the mornings and I looked out across snow-flecked fields to the familiar fells gleaming white and icy in the frosty morning air. But there was another side to the medal. It was too early then to assess the effect of the winter on the hill flocks, but the cold was taking its toll of the wild life on the lake. Each day the Windermere ferryman was feeding the ducks and swans, separated from their food by nearly a foot of ice, and each day he was watching some of them die.

4

Crinkle Crags, Bowfell and Oxendale
Head of Kentmere

I remember, too, lovely March days in 1965. Every morning for days on end we wakened to still mists hanging over frosted fields and fells, the bare trees not even moving their finger tips, and the smoke rising straight from the farmhouse chimneys. And each day remained bright and shining with cloudless skies and the hills asleep in the haze, and each evening the sun went down in a blaze of gold. There were young lambs in the fields and new life peeping through the hedgerows, the lakes so quiet that even an alighting bird could spoil the effect, and the snow still lying in great drifts high in the hills. It was difficult to imagine more perfect weather and yet, earlier that month, the Lake District was supposed to be in the grip of blizzards with blocked roads, villages cut off, and snow and ice everywhere. Unfortunately, the "Lake District" nowadays seems, to some people, to embrace a vast area running from the Northern Pennines to the West Cumberland coast. A few patches of ice on the road over Shap Fell or the usual snowfall near Alston and it will be blared forth by television, radio, and the national press that the "Lake District" is up against it once again, although, as often as not, this is nonsense. During the first six days of March 1965 when the area was reported to be fighting snowdrifts and shot ice, there was no measurable snow or rain in Ambleside but a daily average of four and a half hours of sunshine. And on a day when the "Lake District" was said to be in the middle of its worst blizzard for years, at least one elderly lady in the Ambleside area was sitting in her garden enjoying the sunshine.

March 1961 followed the mildest Lakeland February in memory and you would probably not notice the snow as you drove through the district. But if you knew where to look, you could still find it and up in the Helvellyn range it was lying about ten feet deep in one place, with a good imitation of an Alpine crevasse at the foot of the slope. That year the winter sports season started promisingly enough with several really heavy falls in the hills—although almost nothing on the roads— but then, against all the forecasts, came a long period of mild weather, and Nature seemed to have turned topsy-turvy. By early March the spring flowers were bursting through the ground, but surely with apprehension, we thought, for it was difficult to imagine our reaching April without frosts. But there had been no skating to speak of in the Lake District that winter, and the snow that the skiers were using in the drifts had probably come down two months earlier. In January that year I might have been prepared to discuss the possibility of the snow lasting until next winter—in tiny patches, that is—a situation that had not occurred for a hundred years or more (and only then on unreliable authority). But the sudden mild spell changed all that and I began to wonder instead whether the two patches in the Cairngorms—said to be the only permanent snowfields in Britain—would be able to survive that year. But they did.

That March, like many before and since, I had watched the Easter traffic pouring past my house and north-west into the heart of Lakeland bearing the first massed open-air holiday-makers of the year. Cars with bulging luggage racks—but not so many coaches—motor-cycles and bicycles laden with camping gear and hundreds of young rucksack-carrying hopefuls looking for lifts, all eager to forget the streets and all trying to read the weekend promise of the cloud-capped hills. Past the cherry blossom trees, the clumps of golden forsythia, and the banks of daffodils they streamed all through the afternoon and as the sun went down after the morning's drizzle, the traffic seemed thicker than ever. That night they would be sleeping in hotels, farmhouses, youth hostels, tents, barns, and—in a few cases—in sleeping bags in the rain or under the stars. It would not be the Lakeland Easter they had expected weeks before. The long-range forecaster had promised an Alpine Easter and the mountain rescue teams made their preparations for an anxious weekend, but the last snows quickly vanished from the tops, and the skis and ice axes were left behind. Then we were led to expect a sunny Easter with warm, wind-free rocks for the climbers, but that, too, became unlikely. Invigorating days on the tops for those properly clad against wind and weather seemed more probable, and this is how it turned out. Many went into the hills that weekend for the first time that year and once again there were accidents and tragedies. Every Easter it is the same—one holiday weekend the Langdale mountain rescue team were turned out ten times—and so many of the tragedies are caused through ignorance and carelessness.

They opened the new youth hostel on the top of Honister

Pass in March 1963—the highest youth hostel in the district, and one of the highest in the country. From the entrance, the climb into the hills is half accomplished and the nearest summits are only half an hour away or less. The view from the top of the pass, a few yards away from the hostel door, must be one of the most impressive from any road in Britain—the huge crag soaring to the vertical on one side, the mountain wall of the Buttermere fells on the other, and, straight ahead, the steep, winding descent through the gorge with the beck for company, down to the twin lakes and the quiet meadows. It is not so very long ago that horse-drawn coaches went over the pass, for this tourist attraction was continued long after the motor-car had become commonplace on the steepest Lake District roads. Fifty years ago, the cost of the round trip of about twenty-four miles in eight hours was six shillings. Sometimes passengers had to dismount on the steep bits, and on the descent the drivers often used "slippers" or pieces of wood placed under the wheels to control the speed. The "improvement" of the road was only achieved after a considerable struggle which had its repercussions in places as far away as the House of Commons; and even today there are people who scorn to use the tarmac and prefer to walk instead along the rough, grass-grown tracks of the old road. And this, I notice, is sometimes the way of the youth hostellers.

One blustery March day I went out for a walk over the familiar Coniston Fells with my dog for company. The wind was bitter on the tops but half-way up Wetherlam, in the lee of an outcrop of rock, it was warm enough to bask in the sunshine. Two minutes' sprawling rest was enough for Sambo and then he disappeared to go exploring, so that when I was ready to move twenty minutes later he required recalling with a Boy Scout whistle, which I find invaluable on these occasions. Together we did seven of the Coniston hills that day, and at the end I was tired, but Sambo, who, in his scamperings had probably covered twice the distance, seemed perfectly fresh. White, fleecy clouds hung about the Scafells, and by the time we reached Swirl How it had enveloped this summit as well. It was while we were in these clouds that I lost Sambo, but I pressed on to my next top, fortunately cloud free, and got the whistle going again. "I hope nobody thinks this is the mountain distress signal," I thought, but I need not have worried, for, from my rocky perch, I could see there was nobody for miles. Five minutes later I saw Sambo—a tiny, black-and-white speck half a mile away and 500 feet below—and in a minute or two he was again at my side, tongue out, eyes glistening, and tail thrashing the air. But he had to walk to "heel" all the long miles home.

I was writing about my friend, Supt. Robert Walker of the county police one March. In those days he was a detective—a sergeant, I think—and it was of course natural that he should spend his workaday hours in tracking down criminals, but perhaps a little unusual to find him using his leisure in tracking down—of all things—rare mosses. Mr. Walker was then a plain-clothes officer with the look of a successful judge of say, fat cattle, but nowadays he wears uniform. But, even today, when constabulary duties are done he likes nothing better than to scramble up some steep, dirty gully in a remote part of the fells, seeking tiny plants so small that most of us would never even see them. But once he has collected his specimens his work takes on something of the aura of that of a detective of fiction, for he gets to work in a book-lined study at home with his microscope. The beauty of even the smallest wild flowers is apparent to most of us, but the beauty in a tiny shred of moss is only revealed under the microscope when the keen bryologist can study the amazingly varied leaf-cell formations—perhaps one-thousandth of an inch in diameter—and even count the tiny globules of chlorophyll clustered inside them. Here is a new world of beauty, completely hidden from all except a comparatively few enthusiasts. But it is not only beauty which our policeman seeks in his precious hours off duty, but also the thrill of discovery. Four times he has discovered mosses never before recorded in Cumberland, and once he has done the same in Westmorland. Lake District mosses still "undiscovered" had better look out.

4

SPRING MAGIC
April

APRIL brings the annual miracle of spring to Lakeland, the daffodils and the blossom and the tourists. But while the daffodils and the blossom soon fade the tourists are with us, by days or weeks, for the next six months. Until October the National Park is on view to the rest of the world with the locals acting out their various roles. Then we are left alone—to get things into their proper perspective again.

Some years spring seems to come to Lakeland almost overnight. A day or two earlier the ground is perhaps being dried and shrivelled by biting winds, with nothing growing, the becks stilled, and lakes and reservoirs getting dangerously low. For weeks in the early part of 1964 the wind remained annoyingly in the east and north but then, all at once, about the middle of the month, as if prodded by public opinion, it swung into the south-west and the transformation could begin. For the first time for months we had soft rains, bright watery sunshine and new life bursting through the soil. First comes the quick riot of yellow—the daffodils in fields and woods or spiking through still unkempt lawns and a brave show of forsythia in every garden. The Winster valley is one place to see the daffodils— tens of thousands of them crowding every corner. But here and there in 1965 in the same quiet byways you would see notices by the side of the road telling you that all this loveliness would be drowned and lost for ever if the idea to turn the dale into a giant reservoir is ever implemented.

By mid-April the first of the blossom is showing in places but most of the trees are still without their leaves. Ash, oak and beech remain unclothed but the first delicate shimmering of green is beginning to cloak the birch and soon the dark twigs on a million trees will disappear and the landscape gradually burgeon out in new exciting colour. The hedges, too, take a little time to be convinced that winter is really over. At the beginning of the month the hazel is venturing out but only on a few south-facing hedges is the thorn growing its summer coat while the beech still retains the crinkly ruddy brown leaves of winter, not yet cast off by the new buds.

For the farmer it's a busy time, ploughing, harrowing, manuring and sowing and he must work fast while the rain and wind break up the quickening soil. My farmer neighbour is out early every day with his tractors in the bright sunlight, and as the new brown soil moves richly under plough and rake a thousand seagulls wheel above the stubble, eager for the worms. About this time the sheep disappear from the field behind my house to be replaced by frisky young Shorthorns and Friesians, happy to be out in the open with the new sweet grass just breaking through. And everywhere on fine evenings and weekends the first lawn mowers of the season are out a-whirring and twice-weekly mowing will now be necessary for those who pride themselves on a neat stretch of turf.

The "bed and breakfast" signs, too, begin to appear in windows in the town and villages and the hitch-hikers thicken on the roads leading into the National Park. The chief warden issues his annual warnings about litter and hundreds of volunteers will be out during the summer trying to persuade visitors to be at least as tidy in the loveliest corner of England as they are in their own gardens. For almost all at once we seem to be dealing with a new type of visitor. The extension of the motorways is now funnelling into Lakeland thousands of people from the Midlands and elsewhere who've never been here before, and some of them bring along city manners. They come, some of them, in fast new cars but not all of them are really interested in the scenery. A few are out for a good time—at anybody's expense; they know nothing about National Parks and care less.

It is perhaps a sober commentary on the British way of life that the National Trust has to spend a great deal of money each

year on the picking up of litter on its properties in the Lake
District. People, you would think, visit these places to drink in
the especial beauty of the scene, but apparently they leave
them more or less covered in orange peel, bits of paper, cigar-
ette packets, and—an increasing menace—camera film cartons.
It is a relief to discover that the Trust is not greatly incon-
venienced by empty bottles, although very conscious of the
near indestructibility of orange peel and the durability and
brightness of the snapshotters' rubbish. Men are actually em-
ployed both by the National Trust and the Planning Board to go
the round of the "beauty spots" picking up litter, while those
equally delightful places that have not yet been "discovered" by
the tourist are as yet untainted by desiccating ham sandwiches
and the almost imperishable greaseproof paper in which they
have been wrapped. Even the popular mountain summits have
to be visited by properly accredited scavengers, and one of the
places needing most attention is Scafell Pike itself. Even higher
than 3,000 feet above sea-level a piece of orange peel will
last, it is thought, about six months and still make a glitter
among the boulders. Banana skins are viewed with less dis-
favour for they lose their colour in an hour or two and disin-
tegrate quickly—but unfortunately very few bananas are taken
on the fells. Dry-stone walls seem to be a favourite repository
for the unwanted contents of luncheon baskets, while a thaw
always brings to light unsavoury relics once stupidly buried in
the snow.

By the middle of April 1962 the last, faded remnants of a
long winter as seen from my study window were two or three
tiny patches of snow hanging just beneath the plateau of the
High Street range. Yet only five days earlier we had been
floundering above Kirkstone top in a foot of newly fallen snow
and spring seemed very far away. It had been an odd winter
that year—more snow than we had had for years and some of
the worst gales in memory, but the fell farmers had not been
badly hit and some of the towns hardly affected. Craftily, I had
managed to get in some sort of ski-ing every weekend in the
first four months of that year but this should not conjure up
visions of sunlit snow slopes beneath bright blue skies. On at
least half the occasions conditions were unpleasantly Arctic

with atrocious winds, and sometimes we had deep, slushy snow and torrential rain. Even the worst days, however, have their happier moments and I still have many memories of the sudden lifting of heavy storm clouds to reveal brown, snow-flecked valleys smiling in the sunshine, or distant winter views across half the Lake District and into Scotland.

That year the April scene was traditional enough—wintry sunshine on the still brown fields, cloud shadows moving slowly across the fells, and peaceful, mirrored waters. But not all Aprils are the same. In mid-April 1951 I could see from my window places in the hills where the snow was still lying in ten feet deep drifts. The great white fingers were slowly creeping up the fellsides and in a week or two's time the only reminder of six months of winter would be the ice in the north-facing gullies, but it had been a grim time. Some sheep farmers, who could only guess at their losses, were even saying that the winter had been worse than 1947, and a walk over the fells could show you what they meant. Everywhere the melting snows revealed pitiful bundles of wool, sometimes horribly savaged by the crows, and if you explored beneath the great crags you would find more tragedies, including some not counted by the shepherds. Those on the open fell were the bodies of sheep, weak and starved by the fruitless search for grass beneath the frozen snow, that had crawled behind the boulders to die. The others were the remains of the venturesome ones, tempted by the sweeter grasses and herbs that seem to cling to vertical places. Perhaps a tiny hoof had been too carelessly placed on an icy ledge, there has been a wild scrabble, and then—the sickening dive over the edge, and, with luck, a quick end.

The sturdy dark, long-maned Fell ponies of the Lake District start to foal about this time of the year. Some years ago it looked as if the few "wild" herds on the Lakeland hills might die out, but nowadays they seem to be on the increase, and, indeed, these short, shaggy natives are becoming quite popular. For, of course, this breed of pony is as indigenous to Cumberland and Westmorland as the red deer and just as deserving—if not more so—of preservation. You can still find a few of them running wild on the fells but most of their cousins have become registered and "civilized" and lead a more normal life down in the valleys in all parts of the country and overseas.

The Fell pony is quite large—possibly only the Highland pony is bigger—and most of them are black or brown with manes and tails grown long and shaggy. Those living on the mountains have an extremely thick coat in wintertime and you will see them out on High Street in the bleakest weather, their coats covered white with hoar frost, but apparently fit and contented. They are very strong and active with well-feathered legs and at first glance look dark, wild and almost fierce but, in fact, are the most docile of creatures.

The Fell pony must be the surest-footed beast of burden in the country and, for its size, perhaps the strongest. Watch one of them tackling a sliding patch of scree, a steep, tussocky slope, or a boulder-strewn bog and you will never see him stumble. It was this balance, combined with their strength, that led to Fell ponies being selected for mountain warfare—hauling guns in difficult country. They can do a hard day's work on a farm or carry a sixteen-stone rider and never put a foot wrong. I have even seen them ploughing. The remainder lead a gentleman's life high up in the Mardale fells or grazing zigzag up the lower slopes towards the top of Helvellyn, while a few are used for pony trekking holidays. Many years ago, before the coming of the railways, one of them ran the Royal Mail daily between Penrith and Keswick and they said you could set your clock by the time he passed through. And years before that Fell ponies, their hooves muffled with sacking, went over the passes by night, heavily laden with contraband.

Years ago there used to be a herd of Shetland ponies grazing high up on the slopes of Bowfell. There were perhaps about forty of these and I would not like to say which is the tougher of the two breeds. The little Shetlands seemed to be completely impervious to the roughest weather and you would find them happily cropping the short, sweet grass, their shining coats streaming with water and rivulets flowing down their noses on the wildest days. When the snow lay in great drifts on the fells they might be brought down to the valley to feed, but normally they remained on their favourite grazing ground 2,300 feet up near Three Tarns. Here, on better days they could munch the tasty turf in the late evening warmth until the sun dipped down behind the wall of Scafell. These Shetlands are no longer part of the Lakeland scene but have achieved distinction elsewhere. One fine little stallion born in Mickleden and bred on the slopes of Bowfell eventually won championships at both the Royal Agricultural Show and the Royal Highland, while another became the mascot of the Parachute Regiment and went overseas to Cyprus.

The cloak-and-dagger men of the fells, the egg-collectors, are sometimes about their bold, bad business in April, a principal reason why there are always fewer young ravens and peregrines in Lakeland each summer than nature had planned. Indeed, the peregrine has, tragically, almost been wiped out in the area. Each weekend during the nesting season at one time these men were roping down overhangs to the wild eyries of these fine mountain birds and pocketing the whole clutch every time. Sometimes they were working for a collector from outside the district, often the eggs were sold for big money, and occasionally the man on the rope was an enthusiast interested only in the eggs, not the cash. The raven nests each year in most of his usual "stations", but we do not hear much of the "red" raven nowadays. This was the fabulous bird that used to nest in a crag in Oxendale, at the head of Great Langdale, almost in the shadow of Crinkle Crags. She came back to the same wild spot or near it, as ravens do, year after year, but, unlike other ravens, she laid red eggs. I have seen, in a lamplit room behind drawn curtains, sixteen clutches of these red-coloured eggs— probably the only collection of its kind in existence. Fifty pounds, I have been told, would not buy just one of these clutches. When the glass lid was carefully taken off the tray I was now allowed to touch the eggs and scarcely allowed to breathe.

The average man or woman from these parts—and many others as well—considers that the best damson in the world is the Westmorland damson, grown in or near the Lyth Valley, that quiet, winding, softly wooded byway which is perhaps the best entrance to the Lake District. At one time you could drive along this lazy road for miles without seeing another vehicle, but one week-end most Aprils the valley will be bustling with visitors come from miles away to see the damson blossom in all its glory on a thousand trees. In a normal year April 18th is about the date when the blossom is seen at its best, but some years, especially after biting east winds and frosty nights, it may be a little late. Some of the blossom in sheltered orchards is often out quite early in the month when elsewhere you can just see bursting buds newly flecked with white. Normally the Westmorland damson blossoms without the leaf, but after a savage winter the leaf comes with the blossom or before it—this happened after the fierce 1946–7 winter—which means that the blossom is hidden and the picture not quite so fine.

One year I asked a weather-beaten man in a big orchard near The Row in the middle of the valley what had delayed the blossom. "Top and bottom of it is," he confided, "t'wind's in t'wrang quarter. Now, if it'd swing round out o' th' east happen we'd git blossom by next weekent. We allus reckon on aboot April 18th but this has been sic a terrible, lang winter with nobbut snar, mizzle, and the like ivvery day it's a wunner t'crops are shapin' at a'."

They say the Westmorland damson was brought over from Damascus by the Crusaders, and for as many years as anybody can remember every farmer and cottager living anywhere near the long limestone height of Whitbarrow Scar has been growing them. Perhaps, indeed, there are more damson trees of this type in this tiny area than anywhere else in the country, Look at any other damson and it is round in shape, but the Westmorland damson—they also grow a few in other parts of the country—is oval. Damson growing can be an intricate business with many snags, but some farmers can produce ten or twelve tons of the fruit and the controlled price used to be £60 or £70 a ton. But I can remember Westmorland damsons being offered at twenty pounds for threepence, and still without a buyer. Which, when you consider the perfect bloom on a Lyth Valley damson and its sharp nutty flavour, is very strange.

Soon after it is light every spring morning an elderly man living alone in a pleasant house near Patterdale is up at a window with his telescope, looking at the fells. As a young man he knew these hills intimately, climbing their crags winter and summer. He knew the ledges where the fox-cubs played, the nests of the raven and the buzzard, the route of the old corpse road into the next dale, the names of the tumbled outcrops and their meaning, and the ways of the shepherds and their sheep.

Then he went away to work on the other side of the world, but although he climbed in many great mountain ranges, among the earth's highest mountains, he often thought of the fells he had known in his youth. And when he retired he came home to live among the Lakeland hills and explore them anew. But a cruel fate has decreed otherwise. He can see the mountains every day as he wished, but the limit of his walking must be his garden gate. But he can still talk to the shepherds at the end of the lane, invite the climbers inside for a cup of coffee, and study, through his old battered glass, the first flush of dawn on the distant crags, the vanishing snows he may never tread again, and the long shadows creeping down through the bracken.

Another old friend, Jack, was also a great lover of the mountains and a hut, high up on the slopes of Coniston Old Man, now stands as his memorial. The hut, nearly 2,000 feet up on a steep shoulder of a rocky fellside faces the mist-wreathed buttresses of Dow Crag where we often climbed together. From below, it seems part of the mountainside, a blur of grey amid a tumble of grey boulders, but if you come closer you can see the debris of old quarry workings, of which it was once, long years ago, a part. In 1953, I think it was, Jack saw the tumbling ruin, facing the crags of his youth, as a possible week-end eyrie where young people might learn something of his own philosophy of the mountains. Each weekend and every holiday he worked on his idea, trying to build a roof that would withstand the gales, hauling huge beams or sacks of cement up the fellside or digging out a water supply. Time and again the roof fell in and we urged him to give it up, but he only worked the harder. Sometimes we would give him a hand and he would proudly brew us tea and tell us how he hoped the place might be ready that summer. But one spring day in 1956 when we thought he had many years of service for others ahead, he died, still a youngish man, his mission unaccomplished. That April I wrote, "The hut stands as he left it, unfinished; the young people have lost their friend", but this was not to be the end. For since then the hut has been completed and now provides shelter and accommodation for the young folk Jack wanted to help. And because of his energy and kindly foresight these youngsters can now explore the hills he loved so well.

The last of Alfred Wainwright's remarkable pictorial guides

to the Lakeland Fells—his seventh—was published, as promised, in April 1966. Mr. Wainwright spends his working life among files and ledgers at an office desk in Kendal but every free hour he is striding over the hills. He is not greatly concerned with valleys and lakes but only with the contours and all that they conceal. Every mountain and hillock must be quartered, measured, photographed, and explored, every faint track followed and recorded, each beck traced to its source and each waterfall, cairn, tarn, quarry, and sheepfold tracked down and sketched. He has spent many patient hours on lonely summits waiting for a gap in the clouds to expose the view, and on many a wild, wet afternoon he has been poking about in long-forgotten mine workings or searching for some old spring. Down from the fells in the evening the task has gone on in the quiet of his study. Working with pen and Indian ink he painstakingly prints out his text, draws his maps and panoramas and sketches his illustrations. A night's careful toil might yield two-thirds of a page, but each evening for something like twelve years the work has gone on. Regularly, the now familiar little guides have been emerging from the publishers—each page an engraving of his own original work without one word of type, even to the cover. It has been one man's way of giving thanks for the great joy that can come from the hills.

I've often written about my mountaineering dog but a few years ago—for the first time—I discovered a mountaineering cat. He was a Siamese called Rikki and seemed to be the constant companion on the fells of a mountaineering schoolmaster from Kendal. But in April 1961, Rikki suffered his first defeat, being repulsed, after a week's siege of the peak, by deep, slushy snow on the upper slopes of Ben Nevis, the highest mountain in Britain. Not that Rikki hadn't trained hard for his first "four-thousander". He'd done several tops in the Lake District without oxygen or other artificial aids and thought nothing of them, but the soft snow into which he disappeared at every step on the upper slopes of the Ben proved a different matter. And the final indignity—quietened with a bromide and carried down asleep in a rucksack—would not easily be forgotten. For Rikki was a mountaineer in the proper tradition, well equipped and accustomed to living off the country. He had his own little sleeping bag for high-altitude camping and on the Ben did his own hunting—of mice—among the boulders near the camp site at 2,000 feet. While acclimatizing himself for the summit bid he would disappear into his own private caves among the boulders and only emerge, tired out and well fed, at bedtime. It was, thought Rikki, a wonderful week—why climb mountains when you can hunt all day?—but his master was disappointed. Although a few days later there came some consolation, for Rikki ticked off Helvellyn by way of Swirral Edge without batting a whisker.

Down the years there have been many happy outdoor days in April. One day when the dales were crowded with holiday folk we walked over the High Street fells and never met a soul. The day began at the car park at the end of the tarmacadam that fringes Haweswater, Lakeland's largest reservoir. You step from the tarmac on to a fellside dotted with grazing Herdwicks and the road suddenly changes from a highway into three tiny tracks zigzagging separately up to the heights. There were few signs at the road end that the lake is artificial for the water that supplies Manchester lay high that day and the modern hotel that replaces the drowned Dun Bull was out of sight round the corner. We had hoped for a sight of red deer on our way up the long sharp ridge to our first summit but they must have been in their sanctuary on the other side of the watershed for we saw neither them nor the peregrine which knows these parts. There were tiny patches of snow on High Street where the Roman legionaries used to march, and where, centuries later, the shepherds had their annual carousals, but no footprints and a pleasing absence of orange peel. Perhaps the Romans knew these fells better than we and their present-day neglect is surprising, for these craggy upland valleys with their lovely tarns must be very near perfection. But even by one of these wild, black pools the hand of man can be detected—a tiny dam, not a fraction the size of the great concrete monster we had passed in the car, but just spoiling the picture.

Another April day we went to Dungeon Ghyll and it's a strange thing but although I've been adventuring in the Lakeland hills all my life I'd never been up this ravine before although it must be no more than half an hour's drive from my home. Not the whole length of it, that is. Everybody knows the waterfall at its foot, but few people seem to carry on through the gorges and up past the cascades to the top of Harrison Stickle. In a quarter of an hour you are beyond the familiar scene and scrambling up a jagged gash in the fellside that looks for all the world like a corner of some wild valley beyond the Khyber Pass. Round every bend there is a new scene—a fine waterfall, better than the tourist one below, plunging into its rock-girt pool, a dark tunnel perhaps, overhung with holly, rowan, and birch, a level turf-carpeted stretch with the beck tinkling among the stones, or a tilted rock garden leaning against the fell with a couple of Herdwicks adventurously grazing on the new heather shoots. Sambo found no trouble with the ravine except once when he slithered down a waterslide, but the crag below the summit proved a little more difficult. It seemed a pity to have to go round by the track just because we had a dog, so we had to manhandle him up on the end of a piece of nylon line. He can get up steep places that would baffle ordinary walkers without the slightest fuss, but five feet of vertical rock defeats him unless it happens to be a stone wall. And on this occasion there was the added snag of ice curtains on some of the slabs. But once we were up the steeper stuff we took him off his cord, and he had been sitting perkily, with lolling tongue, on the summit cairn for minutes before we arrived.

For me, Spring one year came to Lakeland on an April day in the Patterdale hills. We were only half a mile or so east of the main Ambleside to Penrith highway, exploring some new rock climbs in a gill below Angle Tarn—the Patterdale Angle Tarn, not the one under Bowfell—but we might have been far away in the wilds. Joe Wear, the Ullswater huntsman knows the place, but hardly anybody else ever goes here. There are no tracks, no orange peel, no sandwich wrappings, and no noise except the mewing of the buzzards, and the occasional slide of shifting scree disturbed by an adventurous sheep. From our eyrie the only sign of the modern world was, now and again, a motor-car speeding along to Deepdale Bridge—tiny coloured toys seen but not heard. Apart from these, the scene must have looked exactly the same a hundred years ago.

The rock climbing proved disappointing, but the day was perfect for lolling about in the sunshine and arguing lazily

Mickleden with Gimmer Crag from Side Pike

about unimportant matters, for smoking tobacco and eating mintcake, for studying fish and insect life in the tumbling gill, for watching the birds, and for wondering where on earth the builders of Lakeland stone walls acquired their energy 150 years ago. Ten yards away a squirrel slunk across the short, upland turf and scurried up into a sycamore tree, and we fell into a lazy discussion about how high sycamores grew up the fellsides. On the other side of the gill a sheep balanced on a pinnacle of rock, with a hundred-feet drop down to the beck and somebody suggested it might be cragfast. But we were too warm and sleepy to think about rescuing sheep, and it was easy to imagine a route by which it could get itself down. For ten minutes the sheep watched us in disgust—a perfect subject for a colour photograph if we had had the energy to get out the camera—and then it climbed down and went for a walk.

The rowans scattered about the crag face were in bud, and the woods, 500 feet below, a mass of new, bright green. The orange, red and blue of the lichens shone in the sunlight, the rich brown of a newly ploughed field far down in the valley glowed soft and warm, and the square acres of Brothers Water, backed by the dark mass of Red Screes, glinted a Mediterranean blue. Due west, the long summit line of Helvellyn hid from us the central mountains, and just below the summit, we could see two small patches of snow—all that remained of the winter cornices.

Just across the valley, we could look right into the great bowl of Deepdale—surely one of the grandest dales in Lakeland, completely unspoiled, and, except to rock climbers, comparatively unknown. A great sunny basin in the fells guarded by the crags of Greenhow End, and backed by the fine skyline of Cofa Pike, Fairfield and St. Sunday Crag. The pools in Deepdale Beck, where I have bathed, fished and adventured, seemed to have disappeared in the haze, and the gullies on Greenhow End and Scrubby Crag and the great rock faces of Hutaple Crag where we have spent many days exploring, seemed innocuous enough. Strange how distance and sunlight seem to flatten the contours; in wintertime, with a little snow about, these crags look fearsome enough. At our feet Angle Tarn beck gurgled and splashed its way down the fellside, but apart from the square expanse of Brothers Water, this was the only water

5

Above Shepherd's Crag, Borrowdale

to be seen. Not a stream on the miles of bare fellside in front of us, only dried-up gills and scratches down the mountain sides where once there were foaming becks. And so spring came to Patterdale that Sunday—bursting buds and primroses in the hedgerows, meadow pipits in the fields and buzzards and kestrels on the crags, daffodils around the trim little chalets of Low Hartsop, ten hours of sunshine and blue skies.

There was a yellow sunset another April evening just tipping the blue shapes of Bowfell and the Coniston fells, but above the sharply edged ridge line hung grey blobs of cloud like gunbursts and, higher still, dark menacing clouds. It would snow that night over the fells, said the weather forecast, and prospects looked poorish for the holidaymakers seeking warmth and sunshine. I could see them through my drawing-room window —a long line of motor-cars, motor-cycles, coaches and caravans, all travelling north-west hopefully towards the hills. My house stands about half a mile inside the National Park and that day in 1963 they had been erecting a sign just down the lane to inform the advancing hordes that they had at last reached the shrine. Until then, the visitor—if he cared at all—had had to guess the point of arrival, but from that day there would be no mistake. This was the first of the new signs and, appropriately enough, it had been bolted into a huge block of limestone, mounted on a plinth of limestone blocks. For this is limestone country, although two miles up the road it is grey Silurian slate, weathering to green or purple, and further into the fells comes the volcanic rock. And over to the north-east it is the red sandstone and elsewhere the green slate or the grey or the multicoloured lavas, ashes, and breccias. Many more of these entrance signs are being set up, each one in the stone appropriate to the district. Red sandstone, for instance, for the Penrith "gateway". We hope the visitors will notice the signs—and perhaps the stone—and that the few thoughtless ones will realize when they see them that they have come to a very special place.

By the end of April 1965 the hawthorn was out in the hedgerows, the oak and the ash in bud and the bright green of the larches and the first shy traceries of the birch beginning to colour the fells. The rowans, too, were sprouting nicely on the banks of a hundred mountain becks and the beeches throwing off their old brown leaves and spiking new ones for the summer.

Soon the daffodils would be over and the brave show of the damson blossom withered away. But the grass was still not growing strong and the cattle, newly let out into the meadows after their long spell indoors, had hardly enough yet to keep them chewing all day.

The sheep, however, looked content and the lambs were enjoying life. I could watch a dozen of them from my window and they go through the same tricks every spring. They climb in turn to the top of a precipitous bank and practise jumps over the edge, sometimes pushing one another over out of sheer *joie de vivre*. As they jump they kick their back legs high in the air and sometimes, to their astonishment, achieve somersaults. Then they all troop up the bank for another go. When they tire of this they climb a low stone wall into another field and have relay races down the edge of the ploughed land, until they get hungry and run off, bleating, to find mother. It must be a great life.

The curlew with its mournful note is out in the stubble field each morning, and each evening at that time the sun was going down in a blaze of gold. Summer was well on the way but a few patches of snow still clung to the higher fells and there might be night frosts still to come. But the Lake District could rest awhile for a few weeks before the next invasion when the trees would be in full leaf and the spring miracle forgotten.

5

A SUMMER AWAKENING
May

THE lovely green bowl of Mickleden in Langdale was filled with noise—the pleasant, homely noise of hundreds of sheep and their newly-born lambs. Now and again a deep-throated "baa" would sound close at hand, followed by a plaintive note in a higher key from half a mile away across the intake fields; then, perhaps a few rather mournful chords, a jumble of discords from the other side of the beck, a peremptory command to her offspring from some impatient old ewe, and all the time a chorus of high-pitched bleating from the lambs. As the evening shadows crept along the close-cropped turf the lambs seemed at their noisiest and friskiest, enjoying their last hour before sleep—just like youngsters—with games on the grass or "follow my leader" over the gap in the old stone wall. The little, clumsy bundles of wool, most of them white with black faces, but a few black all over, fought and jostled with one another, sometimes struggling for possession of a little mound of turf, or trying out the new-found springs in their wobbly legs with high jumps and somersaults. Something like 200,000 of these cuddlesome creatures would have been born that spring— and any spring—in central Lakeland when lambing time was over, most of them unrecognizable from their fellows by you and me but immediately identifiable by their mothers, and even, in a few cases, by the farmers themselves.

Sometimes, when May comes round we seem to jump into summer almost overnight. One morning, after weeks of cold east winds or heavy rain we find that the harsh wintry sunshine has given way to a new warm glow and everything suddenly looks radiant. Everywhere, on the fells, in the fields, and in the lanes are new, luscious greens, the trim gardens overlooking the quiet lakes are ablaze with brilliant colour, and, as we relish the sun on our faces, we feel for the first time that the earth has really burst forth into rich, new life. And, side by side with the new bounty of the earth, there is the sudden awakening of the life of the countryside. Any day now there will be the "Merrie England" pageantry of the May festivals in Langdale and Hawkshead, folk-dancing, perhaps, on a sunlit lawn at Grasmere under the shadow of Silver Howe, and the villages opening their summer "season" with the wrestling, fell racing, and hound trailing of the annual sports. While on a score of new-mown cricket pitches set among the fells there will be the click of bat on ball throughout a long, drowsy afternoon. In the twisting village streets the lassies are out for the first time in their bright coloured frocks, and by the week-end, if the weather holds, the fells will be alive with sunburned climbers and walkers, while the lakes, and even some of the lonelier tarns, may be ringing with the laughter of bathers taking their first dip of the year.

From my window on many a May evening I can watch, although they are two miles away, the moving specks of cars and lorries, caught by the sunlight, as they crawl past the chequered fields towards Scotland. In the foreground are sloping meadows, little copses, and whitewashed farmsteads nestling in the hollows, and, beyond the grazing sheep and cattle, a railway line curving round the contours. But in this rising landscape of slanting fields, straggling woods, old stone walls, low, rounded fells, and, on the skyline, the sleeping hills, the railway becomes completely insignificant, and you may sit for hours and never see a train. The river is invisible from here, but we know that it winds beyond the cattle and through a line of trees, where it creeps between the foothills into the long gash of Kentmere which from here seems to point towards the sky. The evening sun shines straight into the picture so that the shadows are hidden and you can see every detail of the nearer fells, perhaps five miles away. I can see the stone wall, like a black thread, leading straight to the top of Whinfell Beacon and pick out the summit rocks and, further along the ridge, the new radio station. At the foot of the fells are the pylons of the grid looking from here like pairs of match sticks, and further round towards the rising sun the long switch-back line of the Howgills. On winter mornings I can look across at these smooth, smiling fells and decide where the snow is lying deepest and which gully might be worth a visit with skis. But on a May morning the slanting sun moving round to the south moulds the range into brightly lit convex slopes separated by shadowed valleys, and you can imagine the springy turf, and the fresh wind across the tops and the long views into Yorkshire.

This is my view to the east, but to the north-west the picture is more remote and exciting, less pastoral but more romantic, for we are looking towards the mountains. Just to the right of an old Scots pine is the long wrinkled line of the Crinkles and the pyramid of Bowfell, with the Coniston fells to the left and the square turrets of the Langdale Pikes rising beyond a straggling hawthorn hedge to the right. And then, peeping behind a great ash that casts his evening shadow across my lawn, is Red Screes, and, further round, the long ridge leading up to Ill Bell and Froswick and the huge bowl of Kentmere with the gap of Nan Bield nicking the northern skyline. Almost always these are blue hills, turning purple towards dusk, and on a fine May evening the sun goes down behind this familiar wall in a flaming pageant of gold, and we wonder where you could see anything lovelier or more dramatically colourful.

Sometimes during the month of May there are glorious hours when the Lake District achieves an almost magical beauty, and all the well-worn clichés—skies of poster blue, clouds like cotton wool, and lakes like mirrors—really come true. It is the sun and the rain that bring out the magic. Often after a soaking day the sunshine melts away the dark clouds to reveal a smiling countryside washed sweet and fresh, with bright colours in the leaves and blossom, rivers in foaming spate, silvery glints on rain-washed crags, and new pools among the rocks. And, when there is further rain on the way, the hills stand out proud and clear with perfect, long-distance views into Scotland or out to sea. One afternoon on our way into Newlands from Keswick we peeped through the still glistening trees into a rain-washed dale flooded with sunlight. With their backs to the sun the fells reared up like purple giants while the grazing sheep, each ringed with golden light, took on a stereoscopic quality as if cut out of cardboard and placed in the foreground. And a red squirrel, munching a coconut on a bird table, shot us a mischievous glance and slithered in a flash into the cool dark woods.

Another lovely May day we were climbing the sun-drenched rocks of Grey Crag above Buttermere and idly watching, between pitches, a mountaineering sheep on the opposite side of the combe. When we first saw it from our climb it was a tiny white speck wandering about disconsolately on a grass ledge below a vertical rock wall. It was obviously cragfast; perhaps it had been there for days. What were we going to do about it? We could abandon our climb and attempt a rescue, or hurry down to the valley and tell the farmer—which would not have been very bright—or leave it to its fate, hoping it might slither off and be none the worse, as they often do. In the end, being lazy, we deferred our decision, and went on with our climb. Half an hour later, while taking in the rope, I saw the tiny speck fall on to another ledge nearly twenty feet below. It had been making various ineffectual sallies from the ledge, both up and down, and in one of these had perhaps misjudged a foothold. But, by no means put out by its fall, the sheep renewed its efforts to reach safety and each time we looked at the distant rock face the speck seemed to be in a different position. Two hours later we happened to see the end of its bold descent—a slither of perhaps a dozen feet on to the screes and a heartening skelter across the fellside. Within the space of a long afternoon the nimble adventurer had safely descended a hundred feet of rock as unaccommodating as a steeple.

Many times I must have been along Moses Trod, the old smugglers' track that runs round the "back" of Gable from near the Drum House above Honister to Wasdale Head, and my diary reminds me of a walk this way with my dog one May day in 1962. Treading this old track and knowing something of its history you notice how it seems to sidle round the contours as if the excisemen were just round the corner. We don't really know what the ponies carried in their saddle bags—whisky, jewellery, silks perhaps, but maybe just chunks of wad stolen from the plumbago mine in Borrowdale. They say that the

Moses who used this route lived in a crude hut in Dubbs quarry at the back of Fleetwith and that he concealed his illicit merchandise in an even rougher hide half way up the north-facing side of Gable Crag. You can still see the remains of this eyrie—some low, tumbledown walls perched precariously on a ledge that looks out over the distant carpet of Ennerdale's dark green conifers—but the only evidence of human occupation I found there that day was a rusty sardine tin. Whether quarry-men and shepherds could reach this place a hundred, two hundred, years ago seems doubtful, but perhaps they swung down into it on ropes lashed to crowbars hammered into the crag. Nowadays shepherds—even foxhunters—would avoid the place.

From the top of the crag that day we could see big patches of snow still clinging to the Scafells, but it was warm work running down the screes. Safely arrived in the gap at Beck Head from which the bold smuggler could survey his route for miles in each direction—if he unwisely travelled by day—Sambo slid into a pool to cool off, while I tried to decide where the excise-men might have lain in wait. But it all seemed far too peaceful and sleepy for an ambush, and we had the fells to ourselves as we wandered slowly back to Buttermere.

I remember, too, another May day when two of us sat on a bilberry ledge half way up the northern end of Gillercombe Buttress and looked out over half the Lake District. A thousand feet below our heels the traffic was jostling round the corners of Honister Pass, but the only sound to reach our eyrie was the music of the waterfall cascading down through the new brackens on the other side of the mountain. The great crag was lit by the mid-day sun, but we kept well zipped-up against a keen north-easter that caught us when we swarmed out of the chimney and on to the face. A peregrine used to live in this crag but was driven out long ago and only a pair of ravens croaked defiance at our intrusion of their sanctuary. Sambo was dozing on a sunny, sheltered couch at the foot of the cliff, watching, no doubt, with half an eye the Herdwicks browsing near the water-fall perhaps a quarter of a mile away. At that distance he would not know them for sheep, but even a grey boulder, until he is close enough for positive identification, seems a fascinating sight to him. But he had been told to stay where he was and,

Pack horse bridge at Pasture Beck, Low Hartsop
The Kirk Stone

like the good dog he is, obeyed. The "back" of Gable looked dark and mysterious, but the highest land in England, two valleys away, had a friendly look—an easy soaring ridge with the familiar huddle of stone on its summit. Other ridges lay, one behind the other, all the way to the horizon, and, here and there, a corner of a lake or tarn shimmered in the heat haze. A line of specks crept slowly down the side of Gable. "Far too many people about," we grumbled as we cast about for a belay to resume the climb.

But that was a few years ago. You've got to know where to go to find deserted crags or fells nowadays, although the top of Pillar Rock is sometimes a reasonably certain sanctuary. On many warm summer's days the top of the Rock is the pleasantest of places for lunch or a nap in the sun. Perched up there, on a couch of heather or a coil of rope, you can enjoy all the advantages of being on top of a steeple without having to suffer the snags. Even the controversial conifers two thousand vertical feet below you look almost picturesque, and you can lazily watch the clouds sailing over miles of distant fells without turning your head. No sounds reach you on top of the Rock, for you are much too high above the tumbling Liza and the waterfalls, and too remote from the sheep and the occasional movement of scree. Even the clatter of other climbers far below and out of sight is quite inaudible. One May day in 1955, however, although warm and sunny up there I found either luncheon or a sleep equally out of the question. The midges, almost Scottish in their determination and ferocity, were in complete occupation. We had seen none on the long walk to the Rock, met none on the climb, and having left the summit with all haste never saw any again that day, but on top they were in their thousands. Pipe-smoke proved completely ineffective and nobody had thought of bringing anti-midge cream for Whitsun in the Lake District. How I wondered did the midges know it was a public holiday and that the noble summit would be receiving more visiting humans than it had had for many months?

Two of us went up the Rock on the anniversary of V.E. Day, May 8th in 1960 after attending the dedication of the bridge memorial in Ennerdale to those members of the Fell and Rock Climbing Club who fell in the second World War. From the top of the Rock we looked down on the six miles of densely

Langdale Pikes from The Band
Larches at Haweswater

packed, dark green conifers—each one of them planted by hand
—and I remember thinking that no Lakeland valley had been
more drastically changed in half a lifetime than the one that lay
below us, reaching out to the sea. Some people say the effect
is ugly, but this is the wrong word; "unexpected" or even "dis-
turbing" might be nearer the truth, for the poet was right when
he asked, "Which is the more beautiful—a young spruce tree
or Bowfell?" We also looked down at the new footbridge that
had become Lakeland's latest war memorial—a matchbox toy,
it seemed, in the middle of a rumpled green carpet. Others had
been on the Rock all day and told us the sound of the hymns
had once come winging up the fells to their eyrie, so that,
although they could not see the ceremony, they had almost felt
they were taking part. It is now one hundred and forty years
since a local shepherd first scrambled to the top of the magnificent, isolated crag. Between his ascent and our latest that day
there had been many thousands of others, but the place remained exactly the same—until you looked down at the view.
Dark, impenetrable forest nowadays where before there was
just the bracken, the heather, the grass, and the sheep.

May is an excellent month for going up into the hills at
night to watch the wonder of the dawn from on high. It was
half an hour after midnight one May day in 1959 when two of
us left our cars in the wood beside Grisedale Beck and turned
our steps up the fellside towards Striding Edge. At first the
moon was hidden behind the pointed peak of St. Sunday Crag,
but as we climbed it rose above the tops and splendidly lighted
every step of our way. Far down in the valley the farm dogs,
awakened by our clumsy steps, began barking, an owl hooted
from the shadowed wood, and the vague shapes of sheep and
lambs moved silently across our path. We trod the Edge and
swarmed over the pinnacles with ease, feeling like pygmies in a
lunar landscape, with black, unseen depths on one hand, an
eerie, cold whiteness on the other, and the moonlit rooftree of
the ridge at our feet. A little later, from the summit of Helvellyn,
we could see the lights of the sanatorium on Blencathra, the
moonlight glistening on the distant reaches of Ullswater, and,
to the left of the Coniston Fells, a glimmer of the sea. The two
hours before dawn we spent in our sleeping bags, drinking
coffee and fitfully dozing, while the orange glow in the eastern

heavens grew steadily brighter. It was just ten to five when the dawn came—the flaming tip of a fiery sun just lifting over the Pennines. We watched the golden ball soar into the sky, felt its first rays, and trotted down Swirral Edge for the run home to breakfast.

We were climbing Great Gully on the Screes above Wastwater one May day and had been examining the remains of the crashed aircraft that litters the lower pitches when we saw the fox, a long, reddish-brown shadow, snaking through the heather and the bilberries below us. The plane crashed into the side of the crag in thick mist several years ago, but it is no place for the trophy seekers. The pitiably twisted wreckage is still scattered all down the gully and no doubt will remain there for ever, while the more accessible remains of a dozen other aircraft that have crashed on the Lake District fells seem to be gradually disappearing. The fox was not accustomed to meeting folk on this particular mountainside for it is a place where neither hunters, nor shepherds, nor walkers ever go, and so at first he did not notice us. Sometimes he disappeared among the bilberry clumps, but we saw him reach the edge of the cliff, look over, and wisely decide to climb back the way he had come. On the way back he saw us, halted long enough to satisfy himself that we were at a safe distance, and then trotted in and out of the rock outcrops, disappearing over a shoulder of fell.

The bilberries, we noticed, were almost ripe and seemed to be in tremendous profusion that year. Whether or not this can be a sign of a sunny summer I cannot say. Hobcarton Crag is one of the places to see the bilberry in wild profusion. They say the red alpine catchfly grows on this splendid, shattered crag high above the massed conifers of Whinlatter—and only, at most, in two other places in Britain—but unqualified explorers like myself may have difficulty in finding it. It grows, they say, on the left-hand wall of one of the gullies but all I could find the last time I was there were hundreds of square yards of bilberry hanging over the ridges and towers like the greenest of carpets. If you looked imaginatively at the spiky crag end-on from a short distance away the place looked rather like a sunken galleon, hanging in slimy seaweed, and rising, prow first, from ocean depths.

The catchfly, which I have still to find, is said to grow

exactly where a vein of quartz and pyrites outcrops the blue-grey
Skiddaw slate so that the would-be botanist must also be something of a geologist, if not indeed a mineralogist. If the latter,
he will be interested to note the reopening of the old mine, just
down to the col and over the shoulder of the fell, where they
are taking out barytes. Not far away, at the end of an old water
cut which has become a nicely graded sheep trod, are two of the
nastiest-looking holes in the Lake District and, at the time of
my last visit, most sketchily fenced. Anybody slipping down one
of these would never come up again, and I have wondered more
than once how many relatives the sheep, lazily cropping the
near-by turf, have lost down these frightful depths in recent
years.

The oldest rocks out of which the Lake District is made are
among the oldest rocks in the world, and oldest rock of them all
is the dark grey, homely looking stone we call Skiddaw Slate.
The great hump of Black Combe is made out of Skiddaw Slate
and so this familiar fell must be a very ancient hill indeed. But
today it looks a very ordinary sort of hill—several tilted areas
of bracken and heather, with here and there a few oddly shaped
rocks, a wandering beck or two and wisps of cloud sailing past
the cairn. I drove over the old Bootle Fell road at the back of
the mountain one May morning. A couple of Herdwicks nuzzling
in the bracken looked up as the car bounced along and then
resumed their search for sweet herbs, and a curlew hopped
impudently across the rickety track. From the top of the
straggling ridge you can see the sea and, low down in the
north-west, the tall chimneys of Calder Hall. How strange a
conglomeration—one of the oldest mountains in the world, a
glimpse of the atomic age, and, at your feet, a mysterious past
that began long years before the dawn of history. Perhaps we
shall never learn the meaning of the strange stone circles and
old burial grounds that dot the moor and we can only guess at
the ancient rites and lonely life that went on up here before the
Bronze Age. Once there was a village on these bleak slopes and
sometimes pitched battles among the boulders, but today we
are left with a few queer stones and an unsolved riddle.

I have mentioned the afforestation at Whinlatter and in
Ennerdale and you can also see some of it low down on the
slopes of Skiddaw. Seen from across Bassenthwaite Lake the

straight lines of the rides through the plantations, the geo-
metric shapes of the sharply contrasted colours of the different
sections of the woodland, and the abrupt horizontal finish to the
conifers below the bracken, sometimes look unnatural and
rather ugly. Some will argue that straight lines don't spoil a
landscape and ask, "What about square fields? Nobody ever
objects to them." It is, of course, true that you only notice the
shape of fields when you look down on them from a height,
whereas the straight lines of the conifers can be seen from
almost any angle. But the State forests of the future, we are
officially informed, will have fewer straight lines than those we
see to-day. Forty years of criticism—not all of it informed—
have had their effect. Today, rides tend to follow the contours
instead of taking the shortest route up the slope, planting lines
are being set obliquely to the roads so that you do not notice
the regimentation, sections of woodland are being provided
with less regular edges, and spiky skylines are being avoided
where possible. One thing should be remembered We are today
only looking at the scaffolding of our State forests, and even the
scaffolding on a new cathedral has ugly, straight lines. Our
children should see the finished job.

We saw the peregrine, a wheeling crossbow of brown and
white, one May afternoon as it flew silently out of the crag
below us, and we spent the next hour searching for her nest in
the hope of a photograph. But I will not mention the crag for the
peregrine nowadays has only the sketchiest of foothold on his
former Lakeland territory, and I must not reveal a possible
nesting place. Swinging down on a rope and a handline we in-
spected all the likely ledges but the untidy heap of sticks where
the young falcons are born eluded us. All we could find were
the perching places, tiny grass-covered ledges on the edge of
the buttress, where the bird had eaten her prey and surveyed
the world above, around, and below her for more. Several
assorted feathers told the story. On the way down from the
crag the air seemed suddenly full of swifts as they darted, like
tiny, black fighter aircraft, catching unseen insects on the wing,
and then, lower down the mountain, it was the ring-ousels we
noticed, as they flashed among the boulders, with their occasional short, sweet snatch of song. Lying in the sunshine, our

backs to a great, brown rock by the side of the beck, we looked back at the crag and watched the buzzards soaring. There were three of them together, and as they slowly circled above the crag, with just an occasional lazy dip of their great wings, they might have been eagles quartering some high corrie in the Highlands. Sometimes they soared silently upwards, borne easily aloft by the rising currents of warm air, and now and again, they glided gently downwards. As they wheeled in slow majesty we caught the glint of the evening sunlight on their wings.

On the opposite side of the Lake District May is still a little early for a sight of the great ocean birds and their eggs on the vertical red sandstone cliffs at St. Bees Head. But the razorbills, the guillemots, and the fulmars are arriving about this time, the last from far across the Atlantic and the others perhaps from the coast of Africa. The cliffs also attract a few cormorants and there are kittiwakes, puffins, rock doves, and occasionally, it is said, a pair of peregrines. On one May visit the cliffs were mostly packed with herring gulls, and as one approached the air was suddenly loud with their clamour and the sky filled with their beating wings. It is an exciting place, St. Bees Head, with its smugglers' tales, its lonely beach, and the great, crumbling precipices. One moment, approaching from above, you are walking along the gentle turf and through the gorse with the blue hills of the Isle of Man straight ahead; the next, you are suddenly on the edge of everything, with the sea crashing on the rocks four hundred vertical feet below.

Driving along a lane near Dockray to the north of Ullswater one fine May morning I came upon a tawny owl sitting jauntily on a garden fence. As he did not fly away as the car passed I stopped, backed up to the fence, and had a good look at him from a distance of about two feet. We sat staring at each other for several minutes and then, getting bored at the sight of my face, the owl flew away, apparently in disgust. Strangely enough I had a second social meeting with an owl—it had never happened to me before—a few days later in a former shooting lodge in Scotland. We were seated round the fire one evening when we heard a peculiar screeching noise at the window, and there was a tawny owl, blinking at the light. When we got over our surprise and as the owl showed no signs of leaving we opened the window and he hopped into the room on to the back of a chair. Half an hour later, after several photographs had been taken, he was still there and we were feeding him with bits of bacon rind. He had apparently been a weakly fledgeling and had been cared for by the people of the house, since when he often came back for food. They called him "Frankie", short for Frankenstein, and in some lights he did look rather frightening. He certainly did at five o'clock the next morning when I was awakened by his screeching and found him perched on the foot of my bed. After a tricky ten minutes persuading him to leave I went back to bed—with the windows closed.

The merry month of May—every other year—is the time for the Mary Wakefield Westmorland Music Festival at Kendal. Just eighty years ago on the lawn of a pleasant country house on the outskirts of the town was born a tradition that has since become almost a way of life in this part of the world—the tradition of music making. The first music festival—the very first of the great competitive festivals in this country—attracted only four quartets from near-by hamlets and didn't last very long; but nowadays the "Mary Wakefield" runs for six days and attracts more than fifty choirs and at least a thousand competitors. For two years children in a score of Westmorland schools, and adults from every village, get ready for festival week, the old market town decks itself out in newly washed bunting and there is a gay holiday atmosphere in the streets. Miss Wakefield, the banker's daughter, would have been happy to know that the festival she started on her father's lawn, on that sunny Saturday long ago, would still be going strong fifty-five years after her death. All the principles she laid down —no money prizes, the importance of sight-singing, the mass singing of the great choral works after the competitions—are still carried out to the letter. Especially would she have been delighted with the children, singing as if their lives depended on it. Children's Day starts very early for many of the youngsters from the remoter valleys, with new frocks and hair ribbons to be fitted, a great scrubbing of hands and faces and a combing of unruly hair before their long journeys. These young people sing naturally and without strain. Perhaps the beauty they see

around them every day and the music of the becks, the songs of
the birds, and the sound of the wind in the crags may have
something to do with it.

They opened the Neaum Crag caravan and camping site high
up above the Langdale road in May 1964. You approach the site
by driving or walking up steep fellside roads, and the tree
cover is so thick you are almost among the chalets and the
caravans before you notice them. To reach the camp site you
have to climb still higher, and you find the tents snuggled
down in little grassy hollows and obviously quite invisible
from any roads or even footpaths. This, they say, is the best
thing of its kind ever achieved by any National Park authority
in this country—secluded holiday accommodation to suit many
types of open-air enthusiast. On the day of the official opening
I found one of the young campers, not at all interested in the
speeches and a little disconcerted at the sea of umbrellas a
hundred feet below, cooking chips over a stove sheltered by a
battered biscuit tin. From his tent flap he could look over the
Langdale Pikes, and a tumbled wonderland of low fells and
woods, threaded by leaping becks, lay just below. Not a house
or a road or even a telegraph pole in sight. "I used to climb,"
he confided, "but I hurt my leg and we're sailing this time, on
Windermere. They turfed us out of one field and told us to
come here. I've always said I would not be seen dead on an
organized site, but this is all right. You can't even see the
other tents. . . . Yes, the view is fantastic, and have you seen
the copper beeches farther down the fellside, and the silver
birches just coming out? . . . No, we don't mind the rain—
we're used to it. If it keeps on I might buy a fishing rod." And
he turned his chips over in the boiling fat, carefully, one by one,
with his knife, and then made room on the pan for two new eggs.

But to the cave-dweller a tent is an affectation and a caravan
or hut a senseless luxury. A cave, they say, is cheaper, handier
for the job in hand, and much more comfortable. Besides, it
doesn't need lugging up the fellside. The caves are underneath
the crags and are used by the younger and more single-minded
climbers. "Crag-rats" they are called—these wild, young acro-
bats—by the superior and secretly envious. Few people could
find their way to these caves for there are no tracks to the en-

Kipling Groove, Gimmer Crag

trances and, for the most part, the bearded adventurers keep their litter under control. The caves, generally underneath a jumble of giant boulders, are paved with turf or bracken with gaps in the walls filled in with moss and a wall of smaller boulders to keep out the wind. For pallet, one of them has a piece of aeroplane fuselage found higher up on the fellside; others have beds of straw or heather. Inside, you may find a petrol stove and a store of food. These are the places where the "crag rats" spend their week-ends—only five minutes away from the foot of the climbs. They sleep, as well as you or I, in down-filled sleeping bags and, like as not, have a morning dip in the tarn before their bacon and eggs. Shopping in the villages they look unkempt and scruffy, but they are immensely fit. The worst of them may be rough and unmannerly; the best are genuine lovers of the open air—young men at peace with the hills.

Before they built the dam across the mouth of Wet Sleddale and began to flood the valley so that Manchester will not go short of water I wandered into the dale on a bright May afternoon. Although from the heart of the dale, on a clear day, you can see the sunlight glinting on the lorries as they come down from the Shap Fells, this was—before the bulldozers arrived—a genuine stretch of untouched Westmorland. Just a long shallow valley winding westwards into the hills, the home of a handful of dalesfolk and several hundred sheep. When I was there that day three sounds only were to be heard—the cries of the black-faced mountain sheep scampering about among the rocky outcrops, the tinkle of the beck sliding lazily through the boulders and the song of the curlew and the cuckoo. A sheep-dog lay sleeping in the afternoon sunshine near a farmhouse dairy, and a few cows were standing ankle deep in the trout stream in the shade of an old pack-horse bridge. The only person I saw in the valley all afternoon was a man tinkering with a tractor high up on the opposite fellside. Here was a valley without a signpost or a bus stop or a litter bin—just the rough road with the farm gates every few hundred yards and then the fell track leading over the pass, and the old blue hills against the sunset.

Two memories of lovely May evenings before I close this chapter. In one of them I am sailing a dinghy on Windermere,

6

Mark Atkinson's monument on Caudale Moor

or, to be more exact, helping a friend to sail his fourteen-footer in a so-called race. The sun still blazed down from a cloudless sky and the blue-lit fells, the woods along the shore, and the trim lakeside lawns lay mirrored in magical perfection on the unrippled surface. Smoke from the houses hidden among the trees soared slowly vertical. A fisherman, waiting for the evening rise, lolled smoking in his boat, his straw hat over his eyes, and, every now and again, two or three miles away up the lake, you could see the flashing white wake of a speedboat, noisily shattering the sleepy silence. Yacht-racing on Windermere means that summer is really here, but as the craft scattered around us, graceful as swans, have barely moved for half an hour it is difficult to believe we are really racing. For some of us, dallying with loose jib sheets and peering anxiously at the limp racing flag, the beauty of the evening does not atone for the maddening absence of wind. The tiller feels lifeless and a match dropped overboard has hardly moved five minutes later. Yet farther down the lake yachts might be tacking strongly and even heeling over bravely, the crew half over the side. Winds reach Windermere after wandering down the many valleys and obey no known laws. To sail successfully on these pleasant waters you must live fairly close to nature.

In my other memory we are sitting on top of Dow Crag after a day on some of the climbs. Darting and diving about our heads in bewildering trajectories, yet miraculously never colliding, the swifts are enjoying the evening meal off tiny flies carried up to the top of the crag by the uprush of air in the gullies. Across the face of the crag, three or four hundred feet below us, an old raven, looking for food, flopped along in his curious, awkward flight and then—conscious that we were watching—did half a backward somersault just for the fun of it. A perfect evening, with the far side of Goats Water still catching the evening sun, so we hurried down for our first shivering dip of the season. Refreshed and lazily smoking, the fisherman grumbled that he was carrying the climbing rope instead of rod and line, for all over the tarn the trout were rising nicely, with tiny "plops" and quickly widening circles every second. We saw no char—those succulent Lake District fish—but we knew they were there, hiding in the shadows by the dozen. You may tempt them with the fly from the boulders on the edge, but

down on Coniston Water or Windermere you go "trolling"
for them—a pleasant, lazy pastime for a peaceful summer
evening. How did the char get into this wild upland tarn? Some
say the monks of distant Furness Abbey carried them up there
long centuries ago.

6

SMILING FELLS

June

HIGH summer may come to the Lakes in early June—sometimes before we are really ready for it. A drowsy heat haze hangs over the fells and the music of a thousand becks is strangely stilled. The grass turns brown, and only the bright fronds of the new bracken show freshly green. The lakes are lower than they have been for months. Hardly a ripple stirs the water some mornings, and you can watch for half an hour in the soft cool of the evening without seeing a single fish rise. The sunburned, shirt-sleeved boatmen do brisk business. Up on the crags the rock climbers feel the heat rebound from the great rocks like sound from a gong. The mosses in the gullies, sodden for eleven months of the year, are brittle as tinder, and the light breeze that now and then rustles along the heights blows the dead lichen and the rock dust into eyes and hair. Many of the farmers are at a standstill. The hay harvest is going to be later than ever and prospects for next winter's fodder are becoming grim. Drowsily the dairy cows stand in the shade or wade belly deep by the lake shores, and even the sheep, unkempt in their unshorn fleeces, look listless as they crop the drying grass. A fortnight's rain is badly needed.

On just such a June day I was crossing Great Gable with my dog Sambo on my way to meet a friend for a climb on the Napes. It was the first time Sambo had been on the mountain. There was not a breath of wind and the searing heat seemed to flare off the fellside as if from an oven. Dust rose in clouds from boots dragging on the screes and the rocks were hot to the fingers. The sun poured mercilessly down on to neck and arms and my load of rope and rucksack seemed twice its weight. "Any water in the spring?" I asked a passing traveller below Kern Knotts and he shook his head. But I knew he was wrong. For even on the hottest day, after the longest drought, this tiny spring seeping out of the bowels of the mountain is never completely dry. And soon we came upon it—a great cave in the rocks, and, right at the back, in the darkness under the roof, a tiny trickle of icy water falling into a pool the size of one's palm. Sambo, who had been gasping with lolling tongue and glazed eyes for the past hour, lay on his stomach and thankfully lapped the pool dry while I caught the trickle down the rocks in a cup. Five hours later after a great deal of ground, level and vertical, had been traversed or scaled, we approached the same place from a different direction. Nothing to tell it from a thousand other corners of the fells, just a tumble of rocks in a wilderness of stone, but Sambo remembered it. And when still a hundred yards away he bounded away down the scree and scampered unerringly into the cave, there to await us, tongue darting, tail wagging, and refreshed, in the cool darkness.

Every climber knows these welcome springs, one of the best of them being the one bubbling out of the rock at the foot of Dow Crag, near Coniston. Winter and summer it is always there and nature has even provided a little cup-shaped trough from which to drink. There's another near the foot of Pavey Ark, one below Gimmer Crag, a third just underneath the summit of Crinkle Crags, and many more, if you know where to look. One of them is even marked on the one-inch Ordnance Survey map—Brownrigg Well, only three minutes' walk from the summit of Helvellyn. Hundreds of thirsty walkers pass this way in summer without realizing that sparkling refreshment is available only a short distance below the track across the stony top. It is also possible to drink from an unexpected supply among the Great Gable summit boulders—a trough of rain water on a flat-topped rock that seems able to withstand the hottest sunshine. Red Screes even has a tarn—containing, it is said, the highest living tadpoles in England—within a few yards of its summit, and so does the rather lower Thunacar Knott in the Langdales. But the springs have the better water.

It is when the fells are so dry, with once merry becks stilled and waterfalls shrunk to a trickle, that foresters have their worries about the fire risk to their growing conifers. Nine or ten years ago, at a time like this, a carelessly flung cigarette-end started a fire that destroyed one hundred and forty thousand trees in the Duddon valley, and thoughtless picnickers any summer weekend could easily wreak similar damage. Critics of afforestation in the dales would, I think, be pleasantly surprised if they had a look at the fairly new plantations on the Dunnerdale Harter Fell. The trees are growing quickly around three sides of the shapely hill, but there is no drab mass of unnatural colour, no regimentation of marching conifers, and no ugly skylines. Instead, you will find trees following the natural boundaries of crag, scree, bracken and bog, with clumps of hardwoods or brightly contrasted single trees breaking up the spruce, and many gaps and ragged rides cleverly contributing to the planned disorder. The rich greens of the beeches and the warm colourings of oak, birch and rowan contrast effectively with the spruce, larch, and pine, and an occasional Norway maple brings a splash of yellow on to the fellside. Above the crowded woodlands the gorse-fringed crags rear towards a broken skyline, while at their foot the river narrows into the rock-girt pool at Birks Bridge where trout glide lazily in the shadows.

The best place to be this sort of a day is deep in one of these limpid pools among the hills, with a waterfall splashing in at one end and a rowan overhead for shade. Preferably, you jump or dive in when covered in perspiration and so exhausted you can hardly walk, but the shock of cleaving the clear, cold water brings you to life again. Down you go between dark, dripping walls of rock, and then, in a second, you are breaking the surface with all aches forgotten, your skin a-tingling, the sun in your hair, and an urge to push over mountains. The Lake District teems with pools, several in all the valleys—Eskdale, Langstrath, Borrowdale and many more—and in the best of them you can become a new man within the space of seconds. But pools bathing should not be tackled with too much deliberation, for the most enjoyable bathes are the unexpected, the casual, ones. You should not set out in a Lake District heatwave for a day in the pools, for if you do, as like as not, the sun will be off the water, or there will be a nasty cold breeze, or the pool will have dried up. No, you carry on with your day on the fells or on the crags and, if you are lucky, just when you are reaching your limits of endurance, you will find your pool. Perhaps the best bathes of all are those captured on a warm, summer's evening, after a hard day in the hills, with the valley, and food and drink an hour's easy walk away, and the sun still shining on the water. Try one, when there's nobody about, and you'll come striding down to the valley like a giant refreshed.

But these Lakeland days of oppressive heat can be followed by torrential downpours. One June afternoon in 1953 when the shade temperature had crawled into the eighties Nature went berserk in one quiet corner of our countryside and within two hours did more damage than a thousand men could do in a week. One moment the Troutbeck fells were baking in the sunshine, sheepdogs drowsing in the shade, and shirt-sleeved roadmen grumbling about the heat as they worked on the pass. Within half an hour hailstones as big as pigeons' eggs were falling out of the skies, huge trees being wrenched out by their roots, boulders many tons in weight crashing down the fell-sides, and great floods carving out new ravines and tearing up walls and roads as they surged, in boiling, brown fury, down to the valley. Nobody who saw the storm will ever forget that afternoon, and although the roads were quickly repaired, and the flooded homes and ravaged fields recovered in time the scars on the fellside will remain for ever. Nearly two and a half inches of rain and hailstones fell in Ambleside in three hours that afternoon—a downpour, stated the official weather report, "without parallel in living memory". But the report does not say how much rain fell on the upper slopes of Wansfell, where the cloudburst was concentrated. It could have been twice this amount. Although it is true that frequently when it is raining hard over most of England, there is glorious sunshine in the Lake District, it is equally true that Lake District rain can be much wetter than any other. Seathwaite in Borrowdale is traditionally the wettest place in England, but higher up among the mountains it can be much worse. Records award Seathwaite the distinction of the wettest Lake District day ever—8·03 inches on November 12th, 1897—and the tiny hamlet can also claim eight of the ten wettest days of the century, but Great Langdale does not lag very far behind. On a January day more than thirty years ago nearly seven inches of rain were added to the torrents crashing down Dungeon Ghyll, and for concentrated ferocity a recent September will take a lot of beating. In the short space of seventeen hours, 6·29 inches of rain fell in the valley, the Great Langdale Beck carved out a new course, and the road was washed away. Dungeon Ghyll must have been a sight worth seeing that day.

These June storms can be over in less than half an hour and yet in that time completely change the appearance of the hills. One June day a year or two ago we were climbing on Dow Crag above Coniston. It had been a hot, stifling day with a steamy haze hanging over the fells and Goats Water so still you could see the minnows ten feet down. Half way through our third climb we heard the distant thunder and decided to call it a day, but there seemed no need for haste. We hardly noticed the sun go in and the sky darken and we had coiled the rope and trotted half way down the screes before we met the wind. A dry, rampaging sort of wind it was, blowing the dust up in our faces, chasing round the corrie and churning the tarn into a whirlpool. The thunder was much nearer now and the lightning flashes much more frequent. Two-thirds of the sky was an angry blue-black and the remainder an ominous-looking orange. We quickened our steps but were only half way across the moor when a vicious jab of lightning almost blinded us and a great crash of thunder directly overhead seemed to rock the fellside. The first rain spattered on the dusty rocks and the quick rat-tat-tat of hail and, within seconds, we were in the middle of a deluge. In its way it was invigorating and even entertaining for once you are wet through to the skin—this took about half a minute—there is no real discomfort. Within minutes the dried-up fellside was alive with a hundred rivers and we splashed down and along them, knowing we could get no wetter, while the torrent poured down, the lightning flashed and the thunder crashed and rolled. A good end to a good day.

This is the time to see the becks and waterfalls—before the flood waters have all run off the fells. The hills may be quiet again after the downpour but in any one of a score of wooded ravines you will find little else but the noise and the water—the roar of the great falls, the urgent surging of the white water through the boulders, the streaming, swishing, and gurgling of a million hurrying rivulets. A wind, born of the crashing waters, comes gustily down the gorge, the air is filled with spray, and a swift zigzags up between the rock walls and out of sight through the rowans that hang over the depths. And yet a few days later these ravines may be cool retreats with the water lazily sliding over whitened rocks, dripping through the ferns, or tinkling among the pebbles. There is much to see by clambering up one of these ravines—the bright-coloured mosses, full of water as a sponge, the smooth rocks fashioned into columns and basins by the water, the tiny beaches with their flat, white pebbles, and best of all, the pools, with their welcome on a hot afternoon.

And sometimes in June a wild wind from the east comes tearing across the hills so that if you are on the crags you have to balance carefully during the gusts and then climb upwards, as quickly as you dare, before the next gale sweeps upon you. The problem then lies in deciding when and where to stop— "here, on this awkward ledge, or can I reach that shelf six feet away before the next gust comes along?" To be caught by the worst of the wind when balancing upwards on toe scrapes can be too exciting for comfort, and the tug of the rope, billowing out like a lasso, doesn't help. I remember many days, one of them on Pavey Ark, when, to add to our discomfort, we were bombarded by stones, dislodged perhaps by some walkers on the summit, that whistled past our ears like bombs. An hour latter, battered and exhausted, we reached the top to meet the real wind—twice as strong as the gusts on the face, so that it was hard work merely to talk on the level. An angry, personal wind it seemed—singling out each of us in turn and trying to wrestle him to the ground. A handful of birds was hurled haphazard across the sky, but nothing else seemed to be sharing our battle. The Scafells looked calm and peaceful in the evening sun, and huge white clouds rolled slowly to the west. And, far below, the glistening black waters of Stickle Tarn looked strangely smooth. We coiled the rope and fought our way, leaning on the wind, down the familiar slopes to the sheltered dale. The larks were singing above Mill Gill and the insects buzzing in the heather. "Nice calm evening," they said down in Chapel Stile, but we didn't want to argue.

They were emptying the intake fields at Brotherilkeld and sending the ewes and young lambs back to the heaf when we came down off Scafell into sunlit Eskdale one evening in early June. Perhaps about fifty sheep, led by a determined old ewe, and most of them with a bleating, black-faced lamb tripping about on still uncertain legs. It is an annual occasion on every hill farm in Lakeland and the easiest job of the year. All the farmer has to do is to open the gate leading to the rake and the open fell, and the sheep do the rest. No shepherds or dogs are required. Unerringly that evening the sheep were on their way to the fells around Bowfell, six miles away, to stay up there all summer in the one area of high land they had known all their short lives—their own heaf. Just one of the inexplicable mysteries of Nature. No risk, for instance, that they would go by mistake on to the Taw House land on Scafell, just across the valley. The speed of their return to their upland home was quite surprising. They trotted up the valley with vigour, even running a few steps now and again, and the lambs, out of the intake fields for the first time in their lives, were hard pressed to keep up. No stopping to graze or to look at the scenery. "They know where the good feed is," said the farmer, "and they're thoroughly fed up down here. Somebody left the field gate open the other day and some of them were away like a shot."

Earlier that day I'd been standing on a jagged jumble of huge boulders below Esk Buttress at the head of the dale with three weather-tanned dalesmen who looked, with their guns and grim faces, rather like Corsican bandits. One of them pointed with his gun, "Sitha, yon's wheer t'cubs hev bin playin'. This is't spot aw reet." Sure enough, a tiny shelf of grass hidden among the rocks had been newly trampled down, and in a dark hole near the fox cub's playground lay the pitifully mangled remains of three tiny lambs. The dalesman wasted no time on words. "Put terriers in, Ben," he commanded, and, eager for battle, three brown, wiry fighters wriggled down into the unknown darkness of the foxes' lair. In the silence, guns at the ready, the men waited for the foxes to bolt, but nothing emerged except little Jeff who popped up from another likely-looking crevice, and disappeared for another search. And for half an hour or more, without a sound, the terriers scurried in and out of the borran far below our feet. Only once, from the distant depths, we heard a savage scuffle and a strangled cry, but whether the little chaps had found the old fox or the cubs or merely one another we did not know. We had to leave the men to their grim, essential task, but later, from half a mile down the valley, we heard two quick shots. Perhaps a dozen lambs had been avenged.

What is the youngest age at which one may take to the hills? One June day in 1958 on the rocky summit of High Crag above Buttermere we came upon a nine-months-old baby boy. He was lying in a weird-looking contraption, something between a box kite and a small rabbit hutch, which was strapped to the back of his determined-looking father. A hundred feet down the steep ridge, on her way to the summit, was the mother with a two-year-old infant hanging, face outwards, from the straps of her rucksack. Neither child was taking any interest in the remarkable view, and, indeed, both looked extremely bored. At intervals the younger child yelled lustily, being apparently happiest when he was being jolted up and down in his cage and strongly resenting his father's well-earned summit rest. I wondered whether either of these children would grow up to appreciate their parents' obvious love of the hills, or whether the effort had been wasted. In the summer of 1965 a mother carried her ten-weeks-old child in her arms to the top of Helvellyn—why, I can't imagine. My own daughter walked over Styhead when she was two, but it was ten years later before she came to enjoy this sort of thing. We took my boy on his first rock climb—Middlefell Buttress—at the age of seven, but it was many years before he asked us to take him on another. Children, perhaps, should be encouraged to love the hills—in their own time and in their own way.

And coming back to the crags after a lengthy absence can be nearly as awkward as starting to climb. There may still be the well-remembered feel of rough rock and the exhilaration of neat, unhurried progress, but the confidence to step up on tiny holds in the expectation of better ones to come and the happy disregard of steepness and exposure may well be lacking. Two of us discovered this truism one bright June afternoon in 1965 when we found ourselves sneaking off to claw our way clumsily up a modest route on Scout Crag in Langdale that a year or two

earlier we might have used for an easy way off, but hardly as a
worthwhile climb. At the top, nerves jangled, muscles tensed,
and breathing a little laboured, we decided to call it a day—and
get into training before our next expedition. Perhaps as a sop
to our wounded pride we decided to walk up White Gill for the
exercise instead of running down to the road, and some time
later were watching two youngsters half our age high up
among the overhangs on a dramatic new route. The rope hung
down in mid-air, feet out from the face, and the climbers were
clinging to the sketchiest of holds but there was no alarm or
even doubt in their reactions. "It's a bit thin, that move," we
heard the leader shout down to his second, "but there's a good
hand-jam a little higher up. Take your time." The appalling
verticality made our climb look like a staircase and we felt a little
envious of their youth, their courage, their relish of severity,
and their contempt for danger. Sadly, we shouldered our old
rope and slunk round through the bracken and the long shadows
for a reviving drink. How wonderful, we thought, to be young
and fit and in the hills on such a lovely day.

Somebody has been writing to the papers denying that Ireland can be seen from the Cumberland coast, and the corre-
spondence has reminded me of a view I enjoyed early one June
morning many years ago. The viewpoint was the summit of
Scafell, the time about 6 a.m. and it was the sort of morning that
makes life really worth while. Five hours earlier we had sat
shivering on a flat rock a little way below the summit, watching
the Lake District peaks riding like yachts at anchor above a sea
of cotton-wool clouds. But now there was not one cloud in the
sky and a magic clearness in the air that made thirty miles seem
like a stone's throw. Criffel, in the lowlands of Scotland beyond
the broad waters of the Solway Firth, must be nearly forty
miles from Scafell, but that morning it didn't look half-way to
the horizon in the view to the north. We could see right across
Galloway to islands sailing in an almost land-locked sea, and
in the middle was the Isle of Arran with the Mull of Kintyre in
the distance. The Isle of Man, across a dead calm sea, looked
unbelievably close and beyond lay Ireland with its coast-line
cliffs, the flat lands behind, and the mountains of Antrim—
almost as clear as the sight of Furness from the top of Black

Combe. We walked a couple of hundred yards across the summit and there, unmistakable, far to the south, were the mountains of Snowdonia.

There's an old man still very much alive in Ambleside—Mr. Lovell Mason, of whose eighty years of skating I've written earlier—who last century set off from Grasmere and walked over most of the principal mountains in the Lake District—including all the three-thousanders—in a day. So there's nothing new in this record breaking. "But they use cars for the level bits now, don't they?" he asked me one day. "There were no cars in my day." I think he was confusing the Lake District record breakers with the Ben Nevis–Scafell Pike–Snowdon people, some of whom are prepared to use anything. I've seen a helicopter come down at Wasdale Head and disgorge mountaineers, fresh from the Ben, in a nice position for a quick scramble up the highest mountain in England. Times change. One recent Sunday in June two young men I met on Great Gable asked me to point out Scafell Pike and a quick, easy route to the top. "We're doing the Three Peaks next Sunday," they explained, "and we want to be sure of the way." I wondered what they were doing on Gable. But, in the days when people had to use their legs, Mr. Mason knew the way about his homeland hills. Before this century began, and forty years before we had a ski club in these parts, he was ski-ing in the Lake District hills on home-made planks tied on with bits of webbing. "A bad winter for skating this year," he confided. "I only got on the ice twice, and Rydal never looked like bearing. Let's hope it's better next year." Then he hopped on his bicycle and rode home with the shopping.

The recommissioning in June 1955 of one of the luxury motor-yachts on Ullswater, all ship-shape and Bristol-fashion with its carpets and chromium plate, was a reminder of the days—before most of us were born—when the only transport on the lake was a sort of galley, worked by half a dozen perspiring oarsmen. Its departure, they say, was announced by the firing of a cannon. But the fascinating story of pleasure-boating on the lakes, by steam or diesel, is largely a Windermere tale, particularly now that the glories of the old gondola and *Lady of the*

Lake on Coniston Water have departed. Much more than a hundred years have gone by since the first of the steamers on Windermere, the original *Lady*, was launched—a long wooden boat, years ahead of her time, steaming along at about nine miles an hour. She was a paddle-boat, like the next four of her successors, and she was laid down among the trees beside the meandering Leven, quite close to where John Wilkinson, who is said to have invented the iron ship, helped his father to make flat-irons. The most beautiful of all the Windermere steamers, they say, was the old *Swan*—the first of the railway boats, launched just after the old Furness Railway brought the line up to the lakeside in 1869. Twenty-five years later the handsome craft sank at her moorings during a storm and later she went ashore in a fog and even foundered at Storrs Pier after a collision, but she is still remembered by old Lakeland folk with considerable affection. And in the summer of 1965 a steam craft that had sunk in Ullswater during a storm two generations earlier, was chugging along on Windermere once again. Modern divers brought her to the surface and months of painstaking work by Mr. George Pattinson of Windermere had restored her to her old glory.

It is about two hundred years since John Wilkinson's crude iron boat was launched into the pleasant, meandering Winster that separates Westmorland from the Furness Fells, and a cargo of peat moss, cut from the marshy countryside where once great forests stood, floated down the stream. No doubt it was a short, unexciting voyage, but whether the two men on board knew it or not it was a great moment in history, for the clumsy craft was perhaps the first iron ship in the world. Years later its designer, the young man at the helm, built bigger ships, invented the blast furnace, and became a very great man indeed, but what happened to his iron ship? For a hundred years or so it has been generally agreed in this friendly, wooded countryside that the hulk lies at the bottom of the weed-choked tarn— Helton Tarn—through which the river flows, and searches have been made for the relic. Workmen have cleared out the river and lowered the height of the tarn so that the surrounding land can be won back for the farmers, but they have never found John Wilkinson's boat. Perhaps, though, it could still be there, hidden in the mud and silt below the waters where the pike play. Long years ago these almost stagnant waters which today the otters know, were tidal, but the coming of the railways and the building of the embankment round the bay altered all that. Part of the river now follows a man-made course, which explains why the unalterable county boundary leaves the middle of the river as it nears the coast and zigzags, for no apparent reason, through the marshes.

Lives have been thrown away for the edelweiss that grows on dangerous cliffs in the Alps, beckoning, white and silvery in its haughty solitude, but last June I bought two nice clumps of it for my rock garden in Kendal market place. They are much better specimens than the faded little sprigs you are offered in the tourists' shops in the Valais or the Stubaital. More than once, newly back from the Alps, I used to sigh for another sight of the gorgeous spring or summer flowers that always enrich the walk down through the moraines to the hut, but nowadays many of us have them in our own gardens, The rich drops of blue that are the gentians, spiking through the turf, the saxifrages, the primulas, the anemones, and the bluebells and a score of others. And even the most exotic of them can be bought at the nurseries at Grasmere. In scores of visits to Scotland I don't think I've ever come upon white heather—really white heather—growing in the hills, but you can buy any amount of it in Westmorland. Indeed, it is grown here by the cart-load for the Scottish tourist industry. But, so far as I know, nobody has ever started to cash in on the plant life of the Lake District to any great extent—Wordsworth's daffodils, the spring splendour of the gorse, the brave show of the damson blossom, and the autumn glory of the bracken. We have our mint cake and our rum butter circulating pretty freely, but little else. But I had forgotten. In 1964 you could buy tins of "Genuine Lakeland Country Air" in many of our inns, but it was a London firm that thought up the idea. And they sold like hot cakes.

The pretty little cottage further up the dale with the rather striking modern curtains and the gleaming car in the pebbly drive is neither a quarryman's house nor the home of a local farm worker or forester. It is owned by "off-comers"—nice people who come up nearly every weekend and spend several weeks in the summer time pottering about the countryside in their old tweeds and sensible shoes. There are scores of these weekend or holiday cottages scattered about the Lake District and they are presenting a very real problem. For the local working folk, just married or perhaps looking for a little place for their retirement, cannot compete with the money these "off-comers" are prepared to give for an old cottage suitable for conversion. And so every half-derelict cottage bought by an "off-comer" contributes to the drift of the local folk away from the countryside. Too many of the disheartened dalesfolk are being forced to seek their fortunes in the cities while the valleys are filling up with the elderly and the comparatively well-to-do. And gradually the flavour of some of the dales is changing. One cannot blame the "off-comers"—real lovers of the area, most of them, and more knowledgeable about it, too, than many of the locals—but it must be admitted that as a community they do not always contribute a great deal to the life of the district. But an attempt is being made to face up to the problem by one non-profit-making society which is acquiring old cottages and smartening them up—entirely for local people. Some of their conversions have been beautifully done— there are some near Skelwith Bridge—and because of the society's foresight quite a few of the dalesfolk have been enabled to live their lives in their own countryside.

Evening, with its long shadows, its subtle colourings, and its freedom from the blaze of noon is very often the best time of the day to be about on the Lakeland hills in June. Sometimes, too, the distant views are much more revealing. We have often seen Ireland quite clearly when we have come down from the crags on a June evening, with the larks singing above our heads and the little black lambs dancing and jumping across the tussocks. From the Coniston Fells you can see Morecambe, twenty-three miles away as the crow flies, and farther south across the bay, perhaps thirty miles away, you can often make out Fleetwood. Somewhere in the Lancaster area the sun glints on a car windscreen and you catch the distant twinkle. Thirty-five miles away the familiar flat top of Ingleborough is unmistakable and much closer at hand you can see the Flookborough sands, the northern half of Walney Island, and the tiny

Longsleddale

spike of the lighthouse monument on the Hoad at Ulverston. Almost at your feet lies the shining blue length of Coniston Water, and the splendour of the picture is often the blending of this splash of Mediterranean colour with the lighter blue of the sea, the green sunlit carpet of the fells, and the richer hues of the crowded woodlands. The turf is springy to your feet as you trot down the fellside, with the beck splashing its way to the lake on your right, and, high up on your left, the ravens circling their lonely sanctuary.

7

The Esk near Dalegarth

7

HIGH SUMMER
July

THEY were bringing down the ewes and the lambs for the clipping. The road through the dale was jammed with a jostling, steaming throng of animals and the air filled with the noise of blaring and baa-ing. High up on the fellside the eager dogs worked in great sweeps, relentlessly backwards and forwards, chivvying down the reluctant sheep. Four dogs, black splashed with white, bushy tailed, restless and iron lunged, combed the craggy fellside, winkling out the sheep from ravines, bilberried ledges, and bracken clumps, while two more marshalled the growing ragged procession down the fell road. The shepherd, brown and perspiring, brought up the rear. Later in the farmyard, with the sheep crowded in their pens, the clipping began. The men sat on benches with sacks across their knees and quickly snicked away, the fleeces peeling off like orange skins. Once tied about the legs the struggling sheep resigned themselves to the indignity with patience and then, looking naked and faintly ridiculous, trotted away in pained surprise to join the others in the intake field. One Herdwick sheep looks very like any other except to its lamb, but in spite of the transformation—and the newly daubed smit marks—it was not long before the youngsters had found their mothers. Tomorrow they'd go back to the fell to seek a living from the sun-scorched grasses.

This was the scene in Buttermere one bright July morning but you can see much the same picture in any of the dales this holiday month. It is a busy, happy scene, this last big job before haytime, and an indication that summer is full upon us at last. What a pleasant, communal affair is a Lakeland "clipping", with every farmer helping his neighbours for miles around and then sharing real country meals in the kitchen when the job is over! Normally the first sheep to be sheared are the rams and the last—towards the end of the month—the ewes. In between it is the turn of the hoggs—last year's gimmer (or female) lambs—and as soon as these scurry away from the shearer's clippers they change their identity and become shearlings. Once the clippings are over the old tup which used to look so massive and fierce that the children kept out of his way is now only half the size and no longer frightening. Before the clipping the ewes looked stolid, comfortable animals fitting well into the homely prosperity of the dale, but now, with their long, spindly legs and slim bodies, they hardly look like sheep at all. Obviously they have lost something and at the same time seem to have acquired a stupid, bewildered look as if shaken by their own metamorphosis, as well they might be. The plump, woolly lambs, having escaped the shearing, look much sturdier than their straggly mothers and hardly the same animals. During the clipping they are herded away from their mothers and the subsequent reunions are just as baffling as ever. There can be no question, after the shedding of five pounds of long, matted, and rather dirty coat, of recognition by sight and the feat is performed by smell alone. Just another of life's little mysteries. The clippings are hard work but good fun while they last. Everybody for miles down the valley joins in, the men at the clipping and marking, the catching and the bundling, and at each end of the dipping trough; the womenfolk making and serving the food and every now and again bringing out something to wash it down. Then at night, maybe a bit of a sing-song with old Benjy giving us a tune on his fiddle, and perhaps a dance or two as well.

But the clippings are nothing like the occasion they used to be with the tremendous meals and the singing and carousing that went on half the night. Some areas had their own clipping songs—the Martindale Sheep Shearing Song, for instance, with six or seven verses and several different choruses, each one singing the praises of sheep and wool. One verse read:

"Now the sheep shearing's over around the gay board
With hearts full of pleasure and glee
We partake with delight of a plentiful board,
Who so blithe and so happy as we?
From our flocks and our herds our consequence springs,
For the Woolsack is next to the Throne
Its freedom confers both on peasant and king
Such as no other country is known."

Hardly good poetry but then it was written more than 150 years ago, but who wrote the words and music I've never been able to find out. But they don't often sing it today and only a handful of the old dalesmen know the words.

Another July occasion in Lakeland is the rushbearing. Only a handful of these colourful reminders of an age when the earthen floors of the churches were strewn with rushes to keep out the winter's cold still take place in this country, and two of them are in Lakeland—at Grasmere and Ambleside. The reeds and the rushes are cut from the lake and the wild flowers and the ferns gathered in the woods and tied into emblems, posies, and garlands. Then the children, headed by the town band, march in procession through the village streets and reverently lay their bearings in the church. Each festival has its own particular features—the gifts of gingerbread or of bright threepenny pieces, the rush-bearing maidens and the maypole, the religious insignia handed down from family to family, the gaily decorated prams, and the rush-bearing sports a day or two later. Nowadays it's a great day for the photographers—particularly those with colour films—and sometimes even for the television cameras. Centuries ago it might have been a really important day, but today it is more of an excuse to show that even if the rest of the world cares to forget these old country customs we intend to hang on to them to the last ditch. Besides, the children can show off their new summer frocks and it's a nice bit of practice for the band.

My principal memories of these happy occasions are of newly washed toddlers standing along the low church wall in Wordsworth's Grasmere clutching lovingly fashioned floral emblems and looking remarkably like angels, of demure young maidens dressed in green holding the symbolic rush-bearing sheet and being marshalled in the sunshine by a crowd of photographers, of the village band proudly leading the procession, and of laughing bonny babies in decorated perambulators. Inside the church—and at Ambleside, it's the same—there's not one empty seat, and the parson speaks to the children and not to the curious holidaymakers crowding the aisles. Now and again some tiny tot starts whimpering while another tries crawling over the pews, but nobody is worried and the parson knows his audience. A few verses of the rush-bearing hymn and everybody streams out into the sunshine again—the kiddies to collect their gingerbread—and another link with the past is more strongly forged.

Sometimes, too, in Westmorland we have a folk-dance festival in July, and now and again—Langdale is one centre—the Morris dancing. Picture a long Lake District lawn, sloping gently towards the lake, and on it perhaps a hundred garlanded dancers tripping gracefully in the evening sunlight. In the shade of the trees a handful of fiddlers scrape out the old familiar tunes, while the spectators loll near the refreshment tent and ponder on the energy of the performance. One festival follows the same pattern as all the rest except that sometimes instead of the lake there is the river, and one year we had it in Kendal, with the fiddlers brought out of their obscurity and placed in the old bandstand in full view of all. High above the arena the ancient castle ruins looked down on a pattern of colour and symmetry that no doubt appeared much the same five hundred years before. How dignified and graceful are the old folk. That old man with the silver-grey hair must be nearly eighty but his step is still light and his manners courtly. Perhaps the young men in their garlands, sashes, and bells look rather self-conscious, finding the leap back into the Middle Ages a little difficult, but what a delightful picture the carefree children make! The spirit of Merrie England caught, for a brief hour or two, on a sunny afternoon in Westmorland.

A strange silence has crept over the dale, for a scorching sun, rarely hidden by even a wisp of cloud, has stilled the music of a thousand mountain streams and the becks slide lazily through the meadows. Even the sheepdogs, eyes glistening, tongues a-quivering, sprawl panting in the shade, thankful that the clipping is done at last. Too hot to think of work today. But come with me through the birches to the water's edge and feel the breeze that has stolen through the rock gorges to the pool. See the dripping mountain plants clinging to the glistening vertical walls, feel the spray, dancing and tossing like a million ice crystals in the sunlight, and peer into dark, inviting depths that have never known the sun. Listen, too, to the roaring of the fall, the splashing and gurgling among the boulders, and the tinkling of the sliding pebbles, for although the dale may be quiet it is all noise and leaping movement down here. See how the churning waters of a thousand years have carved those smooth basins in the solid rock and here, at our feet, have hewn out this black canyon, vertical and slippery, with not even a smudge of lichen. There's only one thing to do—strip, and jump in. Down, down you will go between the dark walls, and you will rise, gasping and invigorated, without even touching the bottom. Now you can laugh at the heat-wave.

That was in Langstrath in July 1955 when it seemed many years since we had had such warm weather for so long. Every-where we saw brown faces and, in the harvest fields and along the roads, the brown, glistening, muscular backs of the work-men. We could not remember a better hay harvest and already scores of fields gave promise of a second crop. A drive along any of the valleys rewarded you with the rich, sweet smell of new-mown hay, and in a motor-boat in the middle of Ullswater one evening the same lovely summer smell came across the water. On the shore shirt-sleeved holidaymakers mingled with Donald Campbell, the water speed record breaker, and his team or sat on the pier waiting for the steamer, but in mid-lake there was no hint of the excitements of speed or of the shrill voices of the crowds. Just a smooth, blue vastness stretching ahead, a duck on the water a hundred yards away looking like a twig, the steep winding path among the bracken on the side of Place Fell, smoke rising from the turrets where a twelfth-century lord had his stronghold, and on the skyline the purple ramparts of the western fells. The duck takes off in fright as we approach, its wings and feet thudding on the water as it gains momentum, and then sweeps in a long arc two feet off the ripples and swishes to rest again at a safe distance. The sun glares down out of an unbroken sky; the only sound is the homely chug of the tiny motor and the only slightly foreign note a distant speck of yellow which we know to be a marker buoy for the speed attempt. While nearer the pier the brown-skinned youngsters, looking like Port Said ruffians diving for pennies, splash away without a care in the world.

July 1921, I am told although I cannot remember it, was a month like this—one of the hottest and most rainless on record, with the grass burned brown and all the becks and gills dried up. Even Piers Gill, the great cleft that separates Great End from Lingmell above Wasdale, was almost dry. Up to that time the gill had only twice been climbed—by men wearing bathing costumes—for in a normal year the many waterfalls present insuperable problems. But that July was so remarkably dry that a party of three men, Messrs. A. R. Thomson of Keswick, W. A. Wilson and A. Walters decided to attempt the first descent of the gill from the "Corridor Route" which walkers traverse on their way to Scafell Pike.

The three men had made their way down several little pitches and were just above the hardest part of the descent when they suddenly came upon a man sitting in the bed of the gill and gazing down the chasm. He was conscious and gradually he was able to tell his story. It seems almost unbelievable but the man, a Mr. Crump of London, had lain injured in that wild spot without food for twenty days and nights. One can only guess at his sufferings and fears, for he must have long since given up any hope of rescue. I think he made a good recovery from his terrible ordeal. Apparently he had lost his way in the mist while walking from Coniston to Wasdale Head on June 21st and somehow or another had got into the gill, fallen twice, hurt himself and then been marooned, unable to get up or down. Search parties had been out on the fells for days and, but for the remarkable coincidence of almost the driest July in memory and the attempted descent of the gill, his body might have lain there for years.

The climbers lowered him out of the gill, and he was eventually carried down to Wasdale Head on a stretcher. Mr. Arthur Thomson, one of his rescuers, was a remarkable man. Although crippled he could swim well and also became a fine cyclist, riding more than 250 miles in twenty-four hours on occasions, and exceeding 10,000 miles a year for ten successive years. He died more than twenty years ago.

The Windermere swimming "season"—swimming the whole ten and a half miles length of it, and, occasionally, there and back, non-stop—comes in July and August. The length of England's longest lake was first swum in 1911 by a Mr. Foster from Oldham—after two or three unsuccessful attempts, it is rumoured, by Captain Webb, the first Channel swimmer—and it was twenty-two years before the feat was repeated. But, to date (1965) the lake has now been swum more than two hundred times by young athletes and comfortable housewives, children and grandparents, clerks, lorry-drivers, business men, schoolteachers, and even twins. One year a Greek army major swam it four times—just for the fun of it, he said—while the record for the two-way swim—twenty-one miles, and as tough a proposition as the Channel—is held by a middle-aged commander in the Royal Navy. It has been swum in good weather and bad, at night, on the back, and by the breast stroke, and it now only remains for somebody to do it under water by snorkel tube or towing the boat. These Windermere swimmers are a tough breed. Some of them seem able to subsist all day on a spoonful or two of glucose and an occasional mouthful of coffee and, at the end of anything between six and twelve hours of swimming, still be fit enough to row the boat back to Waterhead. Every year nowadays the best of them, men and women, race the whole length of the lake, and in 1965 a race for the double distance, there and back, was held. Four people set off not long before midnight but none finished the twenty-one miles, although one of them was the holder of the Channel record. It was too cold, they said, but they'd left it too late, for this race was in September.

The natural rock gardens of the high fells are perhaps at their best in July. Clinging to the precipitous slopes between the outcrops there are fragrant clumps of heather in many colours—including white—patches of bilberry splashed here and there with the ink blobs of ripe fruit, tangles of bracken, perhaps a new sprout of mountain ash, damp beds of brightly coloured moss, a sprig or two of fairy fern, and tiny, shy mountain flowers

Dinghies by Bassenthwaite Lake
Angle Tarn near Patterdale; Helvellyn range behind

peeping out among the rocks. The sight of such a corner in bright sunlight after a shower, with the dull colours of the washed rock richly glowing and a miniature waterfall glinting and dancing through the glistening foliage, is more rewarding than any prize rock garden. No better heather grows in Scotland, but perhaps the Scots boast about theirs a little more. It was just above one of these natural rock gardens that I found one July what appeared to be the only sheep left on the central Lake District fells. All afternoon the shepherds, with their dogs skirmishing in the bracken had been bringing down the sheep for the clipping, but this one had been missed. And instead of the summer music of "baas" from every direction there was just this piteous bleating from an old ewe who had mysteriously lost her lamb and all her friends.

It was in July 1952 that I found my stone axe-head two thousand feet above the floor of Langdale among a tangle of bilberries and looking for all the world as if it had been chipped a week before. Not a sign of weathering on the lovely grey-green surface, the edges still sharp enough to demand careful handling, and just two tiny stains of lichen on one side. Yet the experts tell us this rough fragment of Lake District stone had lain on this scree slope for something like 4,000 years, and that it was fashioned by some hairy prehistoric man not many yards away, 2,000 years before the dawn of Christianity. Probably this was the district's first industry. Somewhere just above this steep, sliding slope of splintered scree—possibly on that platform where chippings have been found and where the squared boulders might have been used as anvils—the Stone Age men had their "factory". These naked craftsmen of long ago probably worked up here near the summit of Pike o' Stickle throughout the spring and summer roughly fashioning their crude weapons and tools, and in the autumn carried the jagged stone over the passes into the more sheltered valleys for polishing and sharpening. My axe-head was faulty and, with several others, thrown away as unfit for export. And that is the real romance behind these axes. They were carried out of Westmorland, and bartered among distant tribes, even with people from across the seas.

Memories of July days on the crags and fells come flooding

Gathering sheep on Shap Fells
Sheep clipping near Kirkstone Pass

in such profusion that it is difficult to single out pictures of particular occasions. Nearly all have been happy, some exciting,
and several memorable, but I will try to pick just two or three
of the more typical. One July day we found the familiar precipice of Dow Crag festooned with laughing ropes of climbers so
that the grim cliffs had about them almost a holiday air. Two
young men who had been camping out the night before on the
fells were attempting the sensational six hours' traverse of the
cliff from end to end. Now and again we caught a glimpse of
them, high up like flies on a picture rail—a leg rounding a
corner or a flicker of rope down a crack. Others were in easier
places, shinning up dark narrow gullies or spreadeagled in the
sunshine across broad, friendly buttresses. A snatch of conversation was wafted down every now and then to the watchers
lunching on the screes, and here and there a whiff of smoke on
the cliff indicated a party taking it easy for a few moments. A
pair of ravens tumbled croaking out of the crag and across the
corrie, and a sudden slither of scree beyond the tarn told of the
passage of a careless sheep. The tarn lay straight below us,
mostly shadowed by the great crag and a little menacing, but
sunlit and inviting in one corner. Two climbers on their way
down to dinner and unable to resist the temptation plunged
boldly in, and we could see their white bodies, like tiny, kicking
frogs, come to the surface and even hear their almost breathless
gasps of exhilaration. When we left for the fleshpots the sun
had dropped behind the crag and two ropes only, barely visible
in the shadows, were slowly completing their climbs. We struck
down out of the shade into the warm sunshine, down through
the scented fragrance of a summer evening.

Another July day I am sitting alone on top of "The Lion and
the Lamb" above Dunmail—one of the few Lake District summits only attainable by the use of the hands—and looking down
on a field near Grasmere completely filled with coloured tents
and caravans. However much one admired the surrounding ring
of fells one's eye seemed inevitably drawn to this garish splash
of colour. The whitewashed farms, the clustered houses and
hotels fitted into the rural scene but hardly the gaily dotted
field; nevertheless, it may well be the pattern of the Lake
District of the future. But down again in lovely Easdale you
could forget the intrusion on the summit view, for could there

be a more serene, more peaceful little valley than this upon a summer evening? That day the hills were blue against the sunset but the valley floor was flooded with sun and light and the beck came tumbling down from the tarn in a long, winding necklace of pools, waterfalls, and tiny, pebbly beaches. The sheep were nosing about among the brackens, the butterflies and the dragonflies busy among the flowers, the jackdaws chattering in their shattered crags, and down by the farm some sunburned boys were turning over the hay. So near to the busy main road with its coaches and petrol tankers, yet in this quiet dale only sleepy contentment and a glimpse of almost untouched perfection. What a place for retirement—if only they allowed people to build houses there. But should they?

One simple July walk was along the Fairfield "horseshoe"—perhaps ten miles through the lanes and over the fells—but once I was past the hedgerows I didn't see a soul all afternoon. Considering that it was a sunny Sunday in the height of the "season" and the walk one of the most popular, well-tracked routes, this was quite remarkable. But even in the tourists' Lake District it is still possible, now and again, to find solitude. Strangely enough, there was little wild life about that day, either—only a pair of ravens, doing acrobatics over Fairfield, a lone buzzard mewing near Rydal, a curlew on a wall just above the intake fields, and a spawn of green frogs hopping about on the edge of a tiny pool on High Pike. A friendly sheepdog followed me for a mile through the lower brackens before padding back for home, and two fine plough horses grazing near the first stile nuzzled in my pockets, but apart from these, only the cross-bred mountain-sheep—not even a Herdwick. A grey ceiling of cloud billowed gently across the 2,000-foot contour, but as I mounted higher a fresh breeze sent it scurrying away and the farthest cairns glowed in a warm sun flooding down out of a warm blue sky. Far below, hidden by a shoulder of fell, lay Grisedale Tarn where once, they say a king's crown was lost, but the southern view revealed England's largest lake, its islands and, way beyond, the sea. The wind buffeted me along the ridge, but below Nab Scar the wood-smoke rose straight from the chimneys of Wordsworth's lovely home and the Vale of Rydal drowsed in the evening sunshine.

There is a valley about six miles from my home where nobody goes—nobody, that is, save the farmers, a few hunting folk, and perhaps occasionally, the curious. Bannisdale is a hidden valley, for a long low ridge separates it from the normal ways of the motorist and tourist, and few people ever walk its enclosing fells. There is no signpost pointing into the valley, and if the guide-book writers knew of its existence they have kept the knowledge to themselves. One July evening the valley looked exactly the same as it must have looked fifty or a hundred years ago—a long, green trough among the fells, threaded by a winding trout river, with two or three lonely farms, a few walled intake fields, a sprawl of woodland where the foxes hide, a maze of crags half-way along the dale, and, guarding it on all sides, the heights where the buzzards soar. There were no cars there but my own, left beyond the second gate where the fell track leaves the road, no people in sight save two brown, old men getting in the hay, and no sounds except the music of the beck, and, now and again, a bleating sheep. Swifts darted above the sunlit track, a curlew sailed across the harvest field, and a rabbit scurried among the evening shadows and disappeared in a flash. Two miles away, the noise and bustle of the main road to Scotland, but here, not a sign of "civilization"—not even a scrap of litter.

Just over the ridge there's another much longer valley, a long straight dale indeed, that we call Longsleddale. You can almost see the whole length of this dale from the main highway towards Scotland and its entrance is little more than a stone's throw away, but not many tourists go up there as it's still, mercifully, a dead end for cars. The main dale is unwinding and narrow, with the hills rising steeply on either side, but at its head an old track winds between the crags that the foxes know, and over a lonely moorland to what used to be Mardale Green before they made the reservoir. There's no pub or shop or bus shelter or roadside advertisement in the valley—nothing but the old church, several farms, a few cottages, and a lazy trout stream which at one place tumbles splendidly into a perfect pool with a shingly beach. Ravens live in the crags and in a little side valley they used to dig out slabs of gritstone for sharpening the harvest scythes. This is unspoiled Westmorland, not yet discovered by the tourists, so that even on August

Monday you may find solitude there, and only once has the march of civilization hit the valley. Many years ago they brought the aqueduct into the dale after tunnelling through the mountains and you can still see the remains of the spoil heaps if you know where to look. And now (1965) they're threatening to bore another tunnel into the valley to meet the growing water needs of the same distant city. Nothing, they say, will be spoiled, there will be no new motor road through the dale, and everything will be restored to its present state. But how can you possibly do all this blasting and boring and hewing and digging in a quiet place like this without spoiling the scenery?*

An edict from Whitehall has directed that a local business man may not dig up the diatomaceous earth from around one of the loneliest of our tarns, Skeggles Water, between Longsleddale and Kentmere. Altogether there are something like 460 tarns in the Lake District—the biggest the size of a small lake and the smallest little more than a pool caught high up among the crags. The diatomaceous earth, or diatomite, formed from the crustaceous remains of minute animal life, and useful nowadays for a hundred commercial needs, may be found around this little-visited tarn that squats on a shelf a thousand feet up among the heather-covered fells. Down in Kentmere they dig it out in great buckets, and the only other similar industry is in the distant Isle of Skye. But our little tarn is now to be left to the birds—the black-headed gull, the shelduck, the little grebe and the great whooper swans that flap noisily in every October and stay until May. Few people pass this way apart from the occasional bird-watcher or fisherman, so that the tarn can be the ideal place for a restful summer's evening. People are unlikely to get rid of their unwanted bicycles, prams, and motor-car tyres within its reedy depths as they have done in the better-known Watendlath Tarn near Borrowdale. But, then, there's no metalled highway to Skeggles Water, and no farmhouse teas for the tourist when he gets there.

The haymaking is over by the end of July in a good year, the hay nicely stored away, packed to the rafters in lofty barns, but

* Sept. 1966. The Minister has now excluded Longsleddale from Manchester's Water Order so that the valley is now safe—for the time being.

often some of it still remains littered about the fields, cut but too sodden for baling, while elsewhere little huddles of baled hay are drying out. The trimmed fields, yellow-green in the sunlight, with long, sharp shadows from the piled bales, give a new, fresh look to the lower slopes of the fells, showing up brightly against the darker green of the pastures and, high up, the splashes of heather and the thickening bracken. In our part of the world the hay is machine baled—spewed out on to the fields in neatly packaged oblongs—but over the Border they still pile it in ricks—a much longer and tiring job. Nowadays in the fell country, with the tractors clattering away from soon after dawn, haymaking is a relatively easy job, but it still needs forty-eight hours of hot sunshine to dry out the hay for baling after it has been cut. The hardest part of the work is the loading of the bales and ideally you need several people for the job, with the youngsters, home from school, stacking the bales on top of the wagon. Haymaking is still a family job with everybody giving a hand so long as there's light enough to see, and the farmer's wife regularly bringing out pies and jugs of tea for the hungry workers.

Charlie Williams lives in the field just over my garden fence and leads a gentleman's life, mostly eating and sleeping. Charlie is a huge young Friesian bull with a ring in his nose. We've always called him Charlie Williams but none of us, not even the farmer, knows why. In the field to comfort him, on and off, are twenty or so Friesian cows, together with half a dozen frisky youngsters, but Charlie's constant companion is a middle-aged matron with whom his relationships are strictly platonic. Twice a day the cows are taken away for milking and sometimes, for days on end, they are transferred to another field, but the matronly one, with the map of Africa on her right flank, is always left behind with Charlie—for company. "We daren't leave him in the field on his own," the farmer tells me. "He'd not stay there half an hour and would soon tear all the fences down. We've got to humour him." They make a most affectionate pair, these two, although I'm assured that it's only company that Charlie seeks. When they tire of eating they just lie down together and look into one another's eyes and Charlie seems oblivious—for the time being—of his splendid young mistresses, munching away rather sorrowfully at the other end of the field. It is Charlie's lordly disdain for the rest of the herd—except when he has work to do—his natural leadership over this sloping corner of fellside, and his friendship with his middle-aged companion, which have so endeared him to us. Twice a day the farm boy comes to the top of the field and calls the cows away for their walk to the shippon but Charlie knows he's not wanted and stays behind quietly with his friend. I often wonder what they say to each other. Sometimes my dog baits him—not very bravely—through the fencing, but Charlie just ignores him. And nobody dares to walk through the field where Charlie Williams is the undisputed lord and master.

8

LAKELAND ON SHOW
August

ALL the world—or so it seems—comes to Lakeland in August, so we put all our goods in our shop window and set out to entertain them. The high fells and the wind in the crags, the lakes, tarns and waterfalls, cool woods and quiet leafy lanes, it seems, are not enough; we must give them something else, something exciting or spectacular or colourful. And so there are the sports meetings, the sheepdog trials, the shows for hounds and terriers, some of the agricultural shows, and, for the wet day, the exhibitions of painting and local crafts. No doubt they started, these outdoor joustings and shows, so that the dalesfolk could match wind and muscle with their fellows or to find out who had the best dog or terrier. But today, and for many years now, the appeal is to the visiting public, and even at the agricultural shows, the farmer does not seem so important as the young leapers in caps and jodhpurs, or the trail hounds.

Perhaps it is at the sports meetings, especially Grasmere, where you can still catch something of the flavour of the real Lakeland, for some of them have been going for a very long time, and have not changed very much down the years. Sometimes they clang a bell or blow a whistle at the start but more often than not there is a friendly loud-speaker announcement wishing everybody a happy day and stating that the sports are about to begin. They are held in many parts of the Lake District, these dale sports that, in some cases, have been

112

Haymaking near Kendal

testing local wind, muscle, stamina and agility for more than
a hundred years, and in August the season is full upon us. Each
meeting has its own individuality—one, for instance, might
have a decorative "sports queen" while Keswick, remarkably
enough, won't have any truck with bookies—but, by and large,
the pattern is much the same. And it is a pattern you will not
see reproduced anywhere else in England—not the complete
picture of the fell running, the wrestling, the hound trails, the
pole leaping, the running, and in more recent years, the cycling.
The first three stamp the event, for these are contests that
belong to the fells and nowhere else.

When they were fell-running, wrestling, and trailing at
Grasmere a hundred years ago the men and the hounds had
much the same names as they have today. The average townsman is staggered that the young lads or dogs can run so far and
so fast over the mountains, but this sort of achievement is bred
in the bone and the dalesman sees nothing remarkable in it.
And the wrestling—huge, hulking fellows dressed up in fancy
tights and throwing one another to the ground as hard as they
can. Surely, think the offcomers, they must hurt themselves?
But these brawny dale lads have been practising the game since
they first went to school and in a few places keep it up right
through the winter, indoor on mats, in their "academies".
They have been wrestling in these dales for hundreds of years—
nobody really knows how it all started—and to some dalesmen
"the russlin" is almost as sacred as the hunting, which is saying
a great deal. So, on many a sunny summer afternoon in August,
we can see on any one of a dozen fields nestling among the fells
the hounds streaming, yelping, towards the bracken, the locked
wrestlers, gravely circling the greensward, and the leapers,
high up, thrusting from their poles. While now and again the
band strikes up with the brave music of "See the Conquering
Hero Comes" and we see the first of the runners down from the
tops come racing into the arena. It has not changed much in a
hundred years. The wrestlers have shaved off their long whis-
kers and the fell runners no longer wear long drawers or
braces, but it is all somehow still a part of old England. And as
we walk about among the crowd and meet our friends from the
dales we feel that this is a bit of our heritage that should last, at
least, for a little while.

8

Head of Longsleddale

The farm lad in Cumberland and Westmorland, particularly if he lives within reach of one of the "academies", doesn't waste too much of his spare time tinkering about with motor-bikes or going into the nearest town. He gets down to his wrestling. For there's much more to this business than mere brute strength. It is, indeed, a highly technical game and a smallish man who knows what he's about can often topple some great, hulking fellow, nearly twice his weight. The secret is to tempt your opponent into a position of apparent security and then, quickly, to get him off balance. To the outsider knowing nothing of the game the slow circling, with the two wrestlers locked together, may seem a waste of time, a playing to the gallery, but it is nothing of the kind. The men are waiting for the slightest sign of relaxed concentration on the part of their opponent, and the moment one attacks the other must be ready with his counter-move. You don't defend yourself in Cumberland and Westmorland wrestling, you counter-attack; otherwise you are down. Watch an eighteen-stone giant apparently squeezing the life out of an opponent four or five stones lighter and there seems only one possible result, until with a deft twist the lighter man catches the giant off balance and they crash to the ground with the big man underneath. A shrug of the shoulders, a quick handshake, and the giant strides away, surprisingly nimble in his stockinged feet, while the winner collects his ticket for the next round. Nothing is predictable, and a grey-haired dalesman of fifty who has merely removed his jacket and boots may well be a better man than a brawny, costumed youngster with sun-burned shoulder muscles and bursting calves only half his age. An ancient sport, a manly sport, and, in these days when betting tends to spoil so many outdoor events, a surprisingly clean sport. There are encouragements, too. A young lad can practise at his "academy" in the winter time, and stand a chance, the next summer, of becoming the "champion of the world" at his weight. And dozens of eighteen-year-olds from the dales have achieved this distinction.

The best heavy-weight wrestler in the Cumberland and Westmorland style since the days—nearly eighty years ago—of the legendary George Steadman is a blond, fifteen-stone giant from the flat lands just north of the fells with a chest like a barrel. Nearly all the great Lakeland wrestlers are farmers or shepherds—and occasionally policemen—but Ted Dunglinson, the present heavy-weight champion of the world (1965) has the rather more modern calling of agricultural engineer. He cannot remember how many men he has felled since his first big victory at Grasmere seventeen years ago, but each season he wins about a score of finals, which means downing a hundred opponents in a few months. Altogether, he must have stretched out at least a thousand men on various fields up and down the North Country—and he's still several years of wrestling ahead of him. The immortal George, who, with his ruddy cheeks, white side-whiskers, and well-rounded paunch, looked like a contented bishop, went on wrestling until he was old and bald, amassing enough trophies to fill a score of sideboards. By now, Ted Dunglinson must have a similar haul.

The greatest Lake District fell-runner of all time is Billy Teasdale, a thin, wiry little fellow of nine stone who spends the rest of his time shepherding sheep in the John Peel country at the "back o' Skiddaw". In 1965 at the age of forty, he lowered the record at Grasmere Sports after many years of victories there—and after announcing his "retirement" from fell-running for two years running. His lungs are so elastic that he generally reaches the summit flag no worse than slightly out of breath and well ahead of the rest of the field, so that he can usually afford to take it relatively easy on the way down. And when he reaches the tape, with the band playing the brave music, he is no more distressed than you or I might be when we run for a bus. He wears, like all the others, special running boots with short spikes and often a red vest, so that you can easily pick him out, a tiny speck high up on the distant fellside, even without field glasses. But an old photograph of the Grasmere runners taken nearly ninety years ago shows two of the eight competitors wearing low shoes, and all but one of them rakishly attired in what look very like singlets and long underpants, with striped bathing-trunks added. The single exception wears heavy corduroy knee-breeches, a pair of braces, and a powerful beard. Before those days, when seconds were perhaps not so vital as they are today, it is said the runners used to change their footgear on the top, replacing their light boots with a stouter pair.

An August sports day in Lakeland at any one of half a dozen meetings is much the same scene. The green bowl of the sports field may be circled with shady trees and perhaps the old stones of a gracious country house peep through a gap in the higher woodlands. The skyline is the soaring switch-back of the fells. Within the ring of the tightly packed, shirt-sleeved crowd people are dotted about the privileged turf—a handful of officials, a cameraman or two, and the competitors immediately involved. Most of them lounge or crouch on the grass; should they stand up for more than a moment they are yelled at by the crowd, who have paid their money and want to see what is happening. In a shady circle, near the ropes, calmly indifferent to the running, the leaping, and, at some meetings, the cycling, huddle the wrestlers—great sunburned men in white hose and gaily embroidered tights, waiting their turn. The fell-runners are in the marquee near the ambulance tent, massaging their muscles before their scramble to the tiny, fluttering flag on the skyline, and their breakneck descent to the arena. The quiet, swarthy young fellow in the corner, thin as a pitchfork, is the champion fell-runner in England, but the other day, after several years of victories, he was beaten by a wonderful miler from over the Border. "Who will win today?" ask several thousand people—not counting the bookies—but the thin young man, now pinning his number on his back, doesn't seem greatly concerned. A shout goes up from the crowd, and a few thousand pairs of eyes and scores of binoculars are focused on moving specks on a distant fellside. The hounds have been seen, homeward bound with three rough miles still to go, and we wander across to the finish. If it is very hot we feel a little sorry for the fell-runners and the trail-hounds. Especially the hounds who have to go several times further than the men for twice as long, with their only reward at the end—a little bowl of chopped meat, and perhaps a pat on the back if they've won.

But, now and again we see another breed of mountain runner in Lakeland—dedicated amateurs who instead of running up and down one fellside in a quarter of an hour keep up the same sort of thing all day long. In the summer of 1965 Alan Heaton from Accrington ran up and down sixty Lake District mountains—including most of the biggest ones—within twenty-four hours, thereby proving that almost anything is possible these days. In height climbed and descended and distance travelled the feat is something like running up and down Scafell Pike from Seathwaite ten times, but to this should be added the considerable difficulties of navigation since the mountain tops were in mist most of the time. For all this lung-racking labour Heaton got no more than a few pats on the back and the considerable private satisfaction of knowing that, at thirty-seven years of age, he must be one of the fittest men in the country. His achievement came at the end of about a hundred years of marathon running in the Lake District hills, the first recorded feat being a round of the Wasdale fells by a mountaineering parson in 1864. Well-known climbers like the Pilkingtons, J. W. Robinson, Dr. A. W. Wakefield and Eustace Thomas gradually included more and more summits, but when Bob Graham, the proprietor of a Borrowdale guesthouse, managed to cover forty-two of them in 1932 it was felt that the ultimate in physical endurance had been reached. Indeed, this feat remained unsurpassed for twenty-eight years until a new breed of mountain runners led by this same Alan Heaton began, in 1960, to make this legendary record look almost ordinary. The new champion—who got round on jam sandwiches, glucose, and salt tablets—even managed to enjoy the scenery during his long day. He had been lost in the mist on Kirkfell, had fallen on Lingmell and Blencathra, seen the lights of Carlisle from the top of Skiddaw, and had to steer by compass over the Dodds. After a cup of tea and a hot bath at the Old Dungeon Ghyll Hotel in Langdale he seemed none the worse for his exertions but hadn't very much to say. "I think somebody should be able to put in a few more peaks, if they had better conditions," he modestly confessed, "but I'm not trying again." But to improve on this sort of performance a superman, at the very peak of physical fitness —and perfect weather—will be required.

If you go to Rydal sheepdog trials without a dog of some kind trotting at your heels you're liable to feel a bit of an outsider. For this is the Lake District's biggest "dog day", and every August the pleasant meadows between Loughrigg and Low Pike become the hub of a doggy world that stretches from over the Border down to the Midlands. The sheepdogs—perhaps a hundred or so competing in three different classes—are only part of the excitement, for in the judging rings are scores of foxhounds from the mountain packs, getting a little fat during the close season, fierce little working terriers, smooth-coated beagles from a dozen different northern hunts, and sharp-eyed harriers, from anywhere between Windermere and Wensleydale. And when you add to these the trail-hounds entered for the long runs over the mountains and the several hundred pet dogs of almost any variety that always come along it can be seen that this is no everyday affair. Some of these events can attract anything from a score of Masters of Foxhounds—often with a duke or a baronet thrown in—to twice that number, at least a similar number of huntsmen in red coats, and many dozens of dashingly garbed gentlemen who, through long association with dogs and the sporting world, have begun to assume something of the appearance of their charges.

How easy to tell the countrymen from the town visitor! The former, in fell boots and shapeless trousers carries a branch of hazel or, more elegantly, wears riding breeches or drain-pipe check trousers with a shooting-stick, while the townsman has an air of wonderment and carries a camera. Watch, too, how the visitors are happy to sit all day watching the sheepdogs at work and marvelling how they do it, while the countrymen, who see this sort of thing every day, seem uninterested unless they are competitors. But you will not find many of the visitors round the judging ring, where the locals are packed thick behind the ropes, arguing away for all they are worth. "Chanter's ower fat," you will hear one say, or, perhaps, "Yon li'le bitch fra' Patterd'le 'll take sum lickin'. They say she's afeerd o' nowt." Only the hound trails bring town and country together, although five minutes before the visitors have spotted the leading hounds coming home through the woods the locals have seen them high up on the distant fell.

Most people who go to Rydal nowadays know something about dogs, and many know so much that if you could possibly collect all the information together there would be nothing more to learn. But none of the experts who attend this big dog-day seems soppy or sentimental about dogs. A plate of meat for the exhausted finishers at the end of the hound trail, a whispered word of commendation for a particularly successful penning in the trials, or a friendly pat for a first prize at the show, but nothing more. Undoubtedly the dogs are interested in their work—eager to be away in the outrun, or to beat the starter's handkerchief at the trials. And when they've nothing to do they sit and watch the other dogs at work—just as fascinated, apparently, as the holidaymakers, but knowing so very much more about it all.

The competitors at the sheepdog trials look strangely alike. Nearly all wear strong grey or brown suits with no "turn-ups" on the trousers, and very heavy shepherd's boots. Their caps are pulled low over their eyes against the sun and every man carries a stick or crook—the shortest a little longer than a walking stick, and the longest shoulder height or more. Watch a group of these patient men talking together. They are not interested in the trials until their own name is called, but are spending the time talking sheep and dogs—to them the only two subjects in the world—with their friends. At their feet sit their dogs, perfectly motionless except for their twinkling, intelligent eyes, quivering mouth, and an occasional lazy swish of the tail. They have been told to "sit" and they will not move until their master gives the order. Without these magnificent, lovable animals the work of the shepherd on hill farms would be completely impossible. Rightly the French say, "There's no good flock without a good shepherd, and no good shepherd without a good dog."

There are several ways of handling a sheepdog. One is to shout, "Git awa' back" or whatever else you want him to do at the top of your voice, and another is to use a code of fairly piercing whistles. A third is to explain the position quietly to the dog, and then, apart from a little gentle guidance now and again, more or less leave him to it. You will see all the methods in use at sheepdog trials in the fells, but it is the native intelligence of the dog himself that counts in the end. A good dog knows perfectly well that the sheep have to go through those white painted gates and eventually into the pen, particularly if he has seen others covering the same course. If he is an ordinary working dog as distinct from a trials specialist, he may be a little puzzled by the crowds but in general the job is probably straightforward enough. Several times you will notice him taking action—dropping down on his stomach to freeze the sheep, for instance—before any signal comes from his master, who may be too far away to see the position clearly.

Watch these lovely, silken Border Collies in the double-dog stakes. The two dogs will trot behind their master to the start of the outrun, and at the merest nod from him will sit down, one on either side, looking down the course with mouths open, tongues wagging, eyes agleam with anticipation. While they sit there the shepherd talks to them in his own way. He is "showing them the course". There is a whistle from the judges, but the dogs make no move until their master gives another nod. This time they are away, racing along either side of the course towards a bunch of sheep, as yet unseen, in the far distance. They run, perhaps a hundred yards apart, keeping together over rough ground they may not have seen before. Another whistle from the now distant shepherd, heard among a confusion of other sounds, and they immediately halt their headlong chase and lie down, eyes on the sheep they have now spotted, shyly emerging from a clump of trees and scrub. Their movements during the next minutes depend upon an occasional whistle from the lone figure nearly a quarter of a mile away and upon their native intelligence. Slowly, with patience and even guile, they guide the sheep through the "gates" and nearer and nearer to the pen. The rest is sheer magic.

Sheepdog trials have been taking place on Applethwaite Common, above Windermere, since 1891 but the first trials in the Lake District were on Belle Isle, Windermere, in 1877 "before a large and fashionable gathering". And the very first trials in England were held a year earlier in Northumberland, in the shadow of the Cheviot. It has been a long and patient history, this happy blending of the skills of man and dog, and throughout almost the whole of it the central figure has been the Border Collie, the friendly black and white animal with the silky coat and lively eye you will find on almost every farm in the Lake District. Nobody really knows where he came from in the first place, although the Lowlands of Scotland at least three centuries ago were his most likely home, and we can only guess how he came by his superb intelligence. But, today, in many countries of the world, he is recognized as the best handler of sheep ever known and the completely indispensable friend of thousands of farmers.

Sheepdogs—and other dogs too—have nothing like the eye-sight of human beings and it is said they are colour blind as well. Perhaps even a sheepdog doesn't recognize a sheep—at more than a few yards—until it moves; up to that moment it might just as well be a boulder. The last time I watched a Lake District sheepdog trial it was a ragged, little six-year-old with a white patch over one eye, three white paws, and a white splash on the tip of its tail, that won the championship late in the evening when the sun had dipped down behind the hills and nearly everyone had gone home. All he had had to work on to accomplish a feat neither you nor I could manage was his cold spotted nose, his incredibly wonderful hearing, his rare intelli-gence, and his affection for a patient master.

The Lake District show season comes along in August and continues into September. Perhaps it is the first real summer day for weeks and the show field, packed with cattle, sheep, horses, and country-folk, and surrounded by the fells, looks a picture of activity. The cattle are ranged along one side— beautifully groomed cows, sometimes wearing the red, white, and blue rosettes of success on their foreheads, and great bulls chained to the fence through their nose rings, and among them the white-coated cattlemen, quietly scrubbing an animal's leg or sitting down in the straw eating their lunch. One gets the impression they must also sleep alongside their charges; cer-tainly they can give you the history of every beast and its fore-bears, exact figures of milk yields, or the names of champions that have been sired. Across the field the hill farmers are spend-ing the day in and around the sheep pens, examining Rough Fells, Swaledales, Herdwicks, or perhaps Teeswaters with an interest that seems untiring. Nobody else could ever under-stand why the judges prefer, for instance, Joe Grizedale's two-shear gimmers to those of Ned Tyson, but these hillmen know all right. In another corner men are tying garlands on huge agricultural horses or plaiting their manes for the show-ring, and elsewhere hunters are being exercised by bright little girls in jodhpurs and jockey caps. Sporting-looking gentlemen with shooting-sticks are trying to show an intelligent interest in Shorthorns, farmers are grumbling about their hay losses, the bookies are collecting their bets for the hound trail, the refreshment marquee is doing a brisk trade, and the loudspeaker repeats once again; "Will the owner of the little boy in the blue suit please collect him at the secretary's office?" Just another show day in the fell country.

A sunny August is the month when the air is full of splashings, cries, and murmurings of becks, birds and insects, the bracken thickly draped across the hills like a new carpet, and the luscious bilberry harvest there for the picking. How fortunate for the tired and thirsty rock climber that the succulent blue-black berries of this mountain fruit grow mostly on the crags, well out of reach of the commercial picker, for often, after he has belayed the rope on his perch, he can settle down comfortably for a quarter of an hour eating all the bilberries he can reach. Bilberries always seem to taste sweetest when you are sprawled in a bed of them, slung far above the valley and just under the clouds. Sometimes we call them blaeberries or bleaberries, and one also hears of whortleberries, lingberries, or carkeberries. The cranberry, the crowberry, the cloudberry, and the bearberry are different mountain fruits altogether and have little resemblance to the tiny bilberry, that looks like a blob of ink among bright green sheets. Cranberries and crowberries are sometimes picked and sold in Lakeland and the bright red fruit of the cloudberry used to grow near the summit of Bowfell.

But often August in Lakeland is a rainy month and a disappointment to the visitors, especially those under canvas. One of the few things worth doing in the Lake District on a really wet day—a clarty day, we call it—is looking at waterfalls. An even better thing, if you are of the adventurous type, is to climb one. The argument is that having decided to go out on the fells and get wet—without seeing any scenery—one might as well do the job properly just for the fun of it, and have a bit of excitement thrown in. Some routes up Lake District crags are delightfully described in the guide-books as "an ideal wet weather climb", or you can tackle one in Borrowdale where one is assured "The greater the volume of water the greater the difficulty and interest". The only merit of this particular route is that you become drenched through to the skin immediately after starting, thus avoiding the unpleasant ordeal of getting wet through by degrees. Being really wet through is no discomfort, providing one keeps moving. The climbing difficulties are slight, but communications can be trying. Because of the thunder and the crash of the pounding water it is sometimes impossible to hear yourself speak, let alone hear your companion, and when out of sight of each other with the rope churning in the torrent you can savour through the spray the "interest" mentioned in the guide-book.

Once you're really wet through on the fells there's no particular point in turning back for you can't get any wetter and the exercise should keep you warm. It's the process of becoming wet through that's so trying—first the legs and thighs, then the arms and shoulders, and finally, miserably, the back. After that, there's a certain animal satisfaction in splashing through swollen becks or even crashing nonchalantly through tall, dripping brackens. One very wet August day we went into the Helvellyn hills for some gentle exercise. We couldn't see very far, except for a brief moment during a snatched sandwich break on the 1,500-foot contour when the mists slowly parted to reveal a distant stretch of lake and then closed in again for good. Obviously, we thought, there'll be nobody out on the tops today, but on the first summit a patch of yellow turned out to be half a dozen, cheery Outward Bound boys in capes, while around another cairn a mile further into the mist there was a cluster of them, poring over dog-eared maps and fiddling with compasses. "Helvellyn's this way," said one of them to us, more for reassurance than as a piece of information. We agreed, set them happily on their way, and turned down steep runnels of scree into the mist-filled combe above Keppel Cove.

Another August day we had been driven off the climbs on St. Sunday Crag by heavy rain, but on the way down the steep fellside into Grisedale a gleam of watery sunshine shone on the streaming rocks and we stopped awhile to dry off and smoke a pipe. Fifty yards away a young lamb was stumbling about among the boulders and seemed very lame in one foreleg. Repeatedly it would fall forward on the rocky slope and struggle pitifully to rise. We carried it across to some old ewes but they would have nothing to do with it, and the best thing we could do was to tell the farmer in the valley. He didn't seem greatly concerned, and all we got was: "Happen she'll be reet in a day or two." While examining the lamb for a broken leg we noticed the flowers. It is strange that the average man on the fells—unless he is an expert—hardly notices the flowers apart from those immediately around him when he is eating his sandwiches or resting from his exertions. Perhaps this is because many of them are so small. I don't know how many we noticed within several yards of where we sat, but there must have been at least a dozen different kinds—alpine lady's mantle, tormentil, eyebright, thyme, ragwort, mountain harebell, saxifrages, and many more, besides brightly coloured mosses, a patch of heather, and clumps of bilberry splashed with berries. A perfect natural rock-garden and ample reward for a wet day in the hills.

The summer of 1955, my diary shows, was a wonderful time for bathing in the tarns and pools of Lakeland. Warm bathing too—the sort where you can stay in for hours. My last swim that August was in the loop of Swindale beck, which for most of its winding miles had not been much more than a trickle among the boulders for weeks. But at one point, close to some grazing Fell ponies, there was a tempting thirty yards stretch where the shingle dipped suddenly into a long, stilled pool. A shoal of minnows vanished in a flash and a nice brown trout streaked through the shallows as we slithered in. An earlier bathe that month had been along the Westmorland county boundary in the Lune near Sedbergh—twenty feet deep a yard from its canyon-like sides but so narrow that even a poor swimmer could feel safe. We were trying out some amateur frogman equipment and I was seeing the underwater world for the first time. Once under the surface we seemed to be in a vast, silent Aladdin's cave strangely illuminated by an eerie light. The stillness and the quiet were almost ghostly. What little movement we saw—among the weeds, for instance—seemed slow and sleepy. A huge salmon—half spent, we thought—lay motionless in the shade of a rock. We could have got him, had we felt that way, with a pronged spear. A score or more trout zigzagged across the pool quite leisurely as if we were part of the scenery. A few feet away two or three eels wriggled lazily, like the dark shadows of waving leaves. It was disappointing not to be able to stay down in that strange fairy world a little longer.

On the day before August Monday—before they changed the date—two of us went into a quiet dale not five miles away from Keswick and hardly saw a soul from morning to dusk. Three or

four miles away the roads were thick with traffic, while in
Keswick they were queueing in the shops and cafés and the
police were fighting a losing battle with the eternal car parking
problem. More than twenty years ago I had been walking down
this same valley at the end of a day's climbing and I remember
telling my companion that if I was ever able to retire that was
the place I would choose for my home. It was, I recall, a perfect summer's evening and the long shadows were slanting
across the intake fields. The fells and the rocks were clustered
about a tiny hamlet and in the garden of a pleasant, little house,
set among a grove of oak trees, an old man was sitting in a
chair reading a book and listening to the birds. "And that," I
said pointing to the old stone house with its well-kept garden,
"is where I would like to live." "Nonsense," said my more
down-to-earth companion. "That's sheer escapism. You won't
get anywhere by day dreaming. It's unhealthy to think like that
when you're still young."

But this recent August day I had an experience which made
me wonder. Before we went into the valley we stopped at the
last shop to make a purchase and inside I bumped into an old
climbing friend from Harrogate I hadn't seen for seven or eight
years. In a minute or two I had his story. He, also, had loved
this valley all his life and now he had done something about it.
He had bought his dream home there—for weekends, at present,
but later for retirement—and, of all places, it was my old stone
house among the oak trees. "An absolute sun trap," he confided, "marvellous views, all the solitude you want, but civilization quite handy if ever you feel like it. Hardly anybody ever
comes up the dale and the place'll never change. We think
we've been very lucky." So do I, but he had shattered my
dreams. Oh yes, I have a standing invitation to visit them
whenever I like, but it can hardly be my dream valley now. It's
his now, and it's not a dream.

The valley was just the same as it was twenty years before
and for all I know has hardly changed in two hundred years.
You can drive half-way up the valley along a pleasant track and
reach the climbs in another half-hour's walking. A trout stream
tinkles along the pebbles on the floor of the dale and here and
there are deep, shady pools, and, towards the valley head, a
fine waterfall. From the crags that guard the dale you can see

the zigzags made by the miners of centuries ago who dug for the minerals in these parts. Pack ponies had to tread this winding staircase, but nowadays the mines are long since overgrown and hardly noticed. Higher still there is a reedy tarn set in a fold of the fells and unseen until you are a few yards away, and the dale is ringed by green, rock-strewn heights.

The valley points right into the heart of Lakeland and from its head we looked around the circle of peaks—Scafell Pike, with its summit caught in a cauldron of mist and cloud, Gable, proud and aloof, Pillar, with its great crag almost hidden in the shadows, the Helvellyn range, vast and smooth as a whale's back, Skiddaw dappled with sunshine, heather slopes and cloud shadows, the Grasmoor hills, riding the horizon like a line of sailing ships, the Buttermere fells, aggressively shapely, and all the rest.

We finished our climb and walked round the head of the dale. Below the crags a shepherd was working two dogs and even from that distance we could hear his whistles and admire the dogs as they swept the fellside in great circles, bringing the sheep down into the dale. Half an hour later we were back in the valley again and while the dog splashed in and out of a pool we lay on a bank of bilberries eating the purple fruit and watching a pair of ravens doing aerial acrobatics over the crags. Later we drove slowly down the track to the little hamlet, and saw the blue-grey shadows of the clouds chasing across the sunlit fells, two horses with their riders drinking at the beck, and black half-grown lambs playing in the bracken. At the old stone house among the oak trees my friend was hoeing in the garden. He seemed to fit well enough into the scenery.

9

QUIETER DAYS
September

THE new nip in the morning air, the end of the summer bus services up the dale and the lake "steamer" service, the shorter evenings, the garden bonfires, and now the start of the hunting, are all reminders that winter is not really very far away. Mostly, I think, it is the hunting that makes us feel that summer is nearly over, for in the dales the year is sharply divided between the trail-hounds and the foxhounds, with nothing in between. And once you have bumped into a foxhunt or perhaps met a tired foxhound limping home after a hard day there is the unmistakable feeling that there must be an *r* in the month at least, if not a sprinkling of snow on the fells. Official hunting—with the huntsman in his red coat—does not start until October but most of the packs have their first outings in September and the first foxes have been killed while the summer visitors are still with us. By September hounds have exchanged their summer of idleness at the farms for the rather stricter discipline of the kennels and are getting rid of unnecessary fat. And once the packs are knitted together and the hounds as lean as racehorses they will be hunting three days a week—and daily during the lambing season. So that every day during the coming months at least one Lake District fox—and possibly several—will be running for its life, which is not a pretty thought. But the widespread killing of lambs and poultry do not make pleasant news either, and so far nobody, not even the abolitionists, has discovered a better method of control.

These professional hunters—the huntsmen and the whips— are for the most part farmers when they are not chasing the fox. Theirs is a hard enough life and not very well paid, for hunts keep going on only two sources of income—subscriptions and hunt balls. I suppose they enjoy their hunting, for the love of the chase is deeply in-bred in the average dalesman, but I would say that their most noticeable characteristic is their love of animals and not their zest for destruction. Basically, they are dog lovers and half their lives are devoted to the care and breeding of hounds and terriers. If a hound is trapped on a ledge they are prepared to risk their lives to save him. If a terrier is lost down a hole—it happens every season—they will spend days digging him out, going without food or sleep, if necessary.

Nowadays most of the hunts start about nine o'clock in the morning and at the end of a hard day the huntsman and whip have to get the hounds and terriers back to the kennels, feed them and look after any wounds or injuries they might have received. And in the lambing season the day can start at four or five o'clock in the morning and there's hunting every day, rain or shine.

Nobody knows how many foxes there are in the Lake District, but it is safe to state that despite the hunting—and the shooting by the pest destruction societies—there are probably as many as ever. Foxes are prolific breeders and the growth of forestry plantations in the Lake District has provided additional sanctuary for them behind wire fences. The man who often goes into the Lakeland hills will frequently spot a fox if he keeps his eyes open, and I have seen many more of them going about their own business undisturbed than I have seen being chased by hounds. On one occasion while climbing Central Chimney on Dow Crag I saw a fox picking his way across the screes at the foot of the gully and then, a few moments later, a second one. Another time two of us disturbed one of them sleeping on The Screes just as we emerged from the top pitch of C Gully and my dog once chased a fox—without success—all the way down from near the top of Ill Bell almost to Troutbeck Park.

Many of the hounds that will be hunting these splendid little animals—for the fox is a lovely-looking creature—are old hands at the game. Some of them will be running in their ninth or tenth season and these old dogs act as leaders of the pack, for

Campers in Grisedale
Sailing on Windermere

they know better than the huntsman the line the fox is likely to take. All the huntsman can do, once the hounds are away, is to try and anticipate the fox and cut off the corners as much as possible, and it is remarkable how often he is quite close up with the kill.

It is good to see the good old foxhound names coming along year after year—Ringwood, Stormer, Chanter, Charmer, Ranter, Bellman, Dancer, Rover and the rest. Almost invariably they are two-syllabled words, although now and again you get a Bachelor but there was never, as far as I am aware, a hound called True, despite the inaccurate version of "John Peel". The line, of course should read: "Ranter and Ringwood and Bellman so true". One huntsman tells me that a hound should always have a two-syllabled name for the extra syllable can be used to greater effect when calling a hound that is a great way off over the fells. Terriers, on the other hand, often have one-syllabled names; they say that one syllable shouted down a hole into which a terrier might have followed a fox will carry more clearly. Sheepdog handlers don't seem to have any preference. Spot or Fly seem just as effective as Laddie. To most people all hounds look more or less alike but just as a hound trail expert can recognize a hound when he is little more than a speck on a distant fell so, too, can the huntsman. Some of them, indeed, can recognize their hounds by their voices alone.

In September we have the county show in Kendal—10,000 people gauping at a few hundred bored-looking cows, and an assortment of sheep, goats, sheepdogs, leapers, farm produce, and all manner of rattling farm machinery. Everything even remotely agricultural, in fact, except farm horses. Strange that less than one short generation ago the typical picture of a Westmorland farm would have shown at least one horse either grazing in the foreground or ploughing in the middle distance, whereas today the tractor has completely taken over. Sometimes, too, at these shows it is the turn of the tractors in another way—dragging cars and cattle trucks on and off the field, through the quagmire. Recollections of the show are much the same each year—the magnificence of the flower-decked pavilions of the local banks, the frequency with which small boys have to be reunited through loudspeakers with worried parents, the poise

9

Looking across Rydal Park towards Fairfield

of even the tiniest horse riders, the apparent affection of cow-
men for their sorrowful charges, the startling ability of judges
to pick out one sheep from another, and the amount of refreshment a successful exhibitor can consume in one afternoon.
Whether we are countrymen or not we like to appear so on
show day, and so wear our cloth caps and carry shooting sticks.
We even think we know a Shorthorn from an Ayrshire.

The neglected exhibits are almost always the sheep. Thousands of townsfolk may be happy to spend an hour or two
examining matronly cows and huge bulls, admiring Fell ponies,
watching the leaping, or even casting an eye over the goats, but
few bother even to seek out the sheep, penned, almost sorrowfully, in a corner of the field. Only farmers, it seems, are really
interested in sheep, which appear to lack glamour on a showfield, however photogenic they may appear on a fellside or,
with their lambs, in the intake fields. But the hill farmer, once
you get him on to a showfield, is quite content to spend his day
around the sheep pens, and obviously finds the patient bundles
of wool quite fascinating. The lowland dairy farmers, big,
ruddy-faced men mostly, take their turn round the cattle rings,
and, after the judging, go off to meet their friends and enjoy
themselves, but the hill farmers seem to find all the interest and
excitement they require among the Roughs, the Herdwicks, and
Swaledales. Sometimes, indeed, the sheep men look a race
apart—lean, long-striding, quiet-spoken men in fell-boots with
caps pulled low over their eyes and perhaps a crook or a thumb-
stick in their hands, whereas the dairy farmers wear trilbys and
a rather more prosperous air and might even carry shooting
sticks. By and large, then, you only get the experts among the
sheep—men who can tell, more or less, not only whose sheep
these might be, but also, as like as not, what particular bit of
fell they call their home. And only these people know what the
judges are about. You and I can only guess.

Some agricultural shows in the fell country are not quite so
glamorous as the county show. One of them takes place on a
steeply tilted field at the foot of the fells, for there's no level
ground in the neighbourhood. When you drive in you take your
car to the top of the slope for you know that if it rains—as it
generally does—you'll never get out on the level, except at the
end of the tractor rope. But by sliding downhill through the mire

you might just manage it. This is essentially a farmers' show—
no trade stands or fancy marquees or side-shows or youngsters
jumping ponies. Just the cows and the sheep and, almost apolo-
getically, the sheepdogs. Oh, and a bit of wrestling some years,
in case there might be strangers uninterested in Shorthorns and
Roughs. There's not even a notice on the main road to tell
passers-by what all the excitement's about, and unless you happen to hear the man with the loud-speaker calling, say, "Class 22
into the judging ring", you'd drive right past the place. And
only one tent on the field for the president, secretary, judges
and the press, or anybody else who wants to get out of the rain
—that is, if you don't count the beer tent. But to compensate
there's a pleasant absence of restrictions—nobody to tell you
where not to park your car and nobody even to keep you out of
the judging ring if you want to go there. Not to speak of the
best show lunch in the district. It was the centenary show one
recent September but nobody got very excited about it although,
to mark the occasion, the prize-winning cows and sheep were
wearing coloured rosettes instead of bits of cardboard.

At one of our September shows they presented old Jack
Thistlethwaite—"Whistling Jack" to everybody who knew
him—with a walking stick for being "the most remarkable
farm worker in England". He was eighty-seven years of age
then, and had been planting potatoes, cutting hay, spreading
manure, laying hedges, digging drains, and so on for seventy-
seven years. They said he'd never had a day's illness in his life
and was probably the happiest man in Westmorland. On the
day of the presentation Old Jack, a shortish chap with a brown,
crinkled face and looking about seventy, got up early as usual—
he was a bachelor and used to cooking his own meals—and
walked nearly three miles to the farm where he worked, getting
there just before eight o'clock. After about six hours' work in
the harvest field he went along to the show ground in his shirt
sleeves, soiled trousers, and decrepit old hat, and when the
presentation, which he had been dreading for days, was over,
trotted out of the arena as quickly as he could. There were
plenty of people anxious to talk to him, buy him a drink, or
show him round the exhibits, but although it was a lovely day
for idling in the sunshine Old Jack could not be tempted. "I
want to git back to me work," he said, and off he went. His

boss swore he was the best worker he had ever had, and that he
had never given him an order. The old man just stayed on the
job until there was no more work to do, and then walked the
three miles home for his supper. They said he was too happy to
retire, and I believe the old fellow carried on, at peace with all
the world, until he was called to his Maker.

During the long winter evenings or when it's too wet to
work in the fields many Westmorland farmers busy themselves
making crooks and sticks for the summer shepherding, and at
some of the shows and sheepdog trials you can admire the
results of their labours. I don't know whether these shows of
shepherds' sticks are held outside Lakeland but they have been
more popular than ever in these parts in recent years. The staff
that identifies the hill shepherd from the lad who hoes the turnips down in the fields can be anything from a magnificent
specimen five feet along with polished horn crook carved into
a snake or a dog's head to a simple stick with handle trimmed to
workmanlike dimensions. Experts will tell you that the horn
of an old Herdwick ram is the best for making a really good
crook. You cut a likely-looking horn from a carcase, boil it in a
pan of water to soften it, bend it to the required shape, do the
carving and then spend weeks polishing it. In a really first-
class job the colours shine out clearly and the surface is as bright
as cut glass. To make a wooden stick you simply cut your
chosen ash or hazel low down at the bole and then carve it to
any shape you fancy. No shepherd would be without his stick or
crook, particularly at lambing time, and most of them have
half a dozen stacked just inside the porch.

One bright September morning we were called out to rescue
a ewe marooned on a sloping ledge twelve feet long and perhaps three feet wide overlooking a rather nasty precipice in
Kentmere. She had been there for nearly a fortnight. When she
had first slithered down to the ledge in her search for sweet
herbs, heather roots, and bilberries it had been thickly carpeted
with succulent grazing. Now, ever blade of grass had been
desperately cropped almost down to the rock and the ledge
had become a bare mass of brown earth, trampled hard. Her
rescue from above involved a certain amount of rope acrobatics,
the offer of a bait, and a wrestling match in rather restricted

circumstances. Sheep are well known for their stupidity, but their apparent preference for a quick death rather than deliverance by unknown hands is the baffling feature of any rescue. They are surer-footed on a craggy fellside than most humans, but while they can descend, by balancing or slithering, remarkably steep pitches, they are relatively poor at climbing "up-bank", as we say in Westmorland. As a result they are often cragfast above sensational drops but not far below easy ground.

Once when climbing Sandbed Gill above St. John's Vale we found the debris of half a dozen buzzards' nests, some shy rock plants, and the remains of at least a dozen sheep that had fallen from the crags above. The death roll of sheep killed in this way in the fells must total hundreds each year but little can be done about it. Here and there you find short sections of rough walling above the vertical drops, but it is obviously quite impossible to fence off all the hundreds of crags where sheep may wander. And so every week, as the sheep prospect lower and lower in search of the more succulent herbs, there are these little unrecorded tragedies of the fells. Sometimes there may be a misjudged leap, a slither of tiny hooves on slimy lichen, a sickening plunge on to the screes, and a meal for the ravens. Or perhaps a sheep might find herself marooned on a tiny ledge and unable to scramble back to safety. Whether sheep are philosophical or merely dumb I cannot say but there is no apparent panic, no cries for help. She merely continues with her life's job of eating and when she has eaten everything within reach she lies down and waits—probably for days—for the end. The luckiest may be rescued by the farmer or a friendly cragsman but some are hardly missed and, even after death, rarely found.

Inside another Lakeland gully—Great Gully on The Screes overlooking Wastwater—we found besides the remains of dead sheep and bedraggled buzzards' nests, the wreckage of an aeroplane—the echo of some war-time crash. We had gone to the gully hoping to find it dry after the long summer drought but it was wet as ever and greasier than usual. Holds were masked with bright green moss and slime, the water sprayed off the gully walls, and we clawed and hauled our way up cool, dank chimneys in a grey shadowed funnel. Within, everything was wet and gloomy, but outside, framed by the black streaming walls, we could see the lake far below and a segment of a sunlit countryside. And, between pitches, while we untangled the sodden ropes, we wondered at the pattern of the stones around the water's edge or tried to remember the name of the little tarn in the distant strip of fellside.

Not far away, on Scafell, in September 1958 we saw where the savage fury of an electric storm had struck at the bastions of the highest land in England and, in places, torn great gashes in its defences. Thousands of tons of rock had been gouged, perhaps within seconds, out of the mountainside and hurled down towards the valleys. Avalanches of boulders had poured over the precipices, huge sections of fellside laid bare, old becks heaped high with rocks, turf, and bracken, and new gullies carved out of the upland slopes. Nothing could have survived the crash and havoc of the upheaval but probably nobody saw it happen or even heard it. Some of the most spectacular damage, it is thought, was caused by lightning; elsewhere, rain of tropical intensity had altered the face of the mountainside. In other parts of the fells, too, were striking evidence that year of the recent fury of the elements, so catastrophic that it seemed miraculous in a crowded holiday season that nobody had been killed or injured in the storms and their aftermath. Some years ago a visitor had been killed in the cloudburst that shattered a square mile of fellside just south of Kirkstone Pass. But the only casualties of the 1958 storms were sheep and birds and the smaller creatures of the mountains. Slowly the mountains are constantly changing. Every year new becks are carved out of the fellsides and each spring, after the ice has split the crags, there are new rock falls on to the screes.

For many years now the finest of our mountain birds, the peregrine falcon, has been increasingly facing extermination in Lakeland. Although it is illegal to take or kill peregrines—unless you have a falconer's licence—or to steal its eggs, the work of destruction goes on each year and nobody seems to be able to do very much about it. Some of the senior mountaineering clubs have been asked by the Royal Society for the Protection of Birds to report any approach made to their members by egg collectors and also to help where possible in recording their eyries, but nobody in recent years has been caught red-handed, as they have in Scotland, and no police court report has got into the papers. The scale of destruction has been abominable. In 1957, it is reliably reported, only three of the eighteen known eyries in the Lakeland area were missed by the collectors and their hired steeplejacks. All the eggs in the remaining eyries were robbed—first and second clutches in some cases—and of the few young hatched out, several were shot before reaching maturity. Even the device of marking the eggs with indelible ink or dye, in the hope that the robbers would not consider them worth taking, failed. One exceptionally determined bird that produced three clutches on one Lakeland crag had every single egg taken away from her.

In 1962 not one young peregrine, I was reliably informed, had been successfully hatched out on any of our crags although young had been reared in at least one eyrie in the Northern Pennines. There may be something like thirty places in the National Park where nesting is still taking place but if the eggs are not taken, the birds are shot or scattered. The increasing use of the crags by climbers also tends to drive the birds away and gamekeepers and pigeon fanciers are their sworn enemies. Sometimes the young birds are taken out of the crags for sale to falconers who train them for sport. Peregrines, too, are sometimes killed unwittingly by the farmers. The falcon lives and feeds its young on smaller birds, including the pigeon, that feed on grain, weeds, and other greenstuff which has often been contaminated by poisonous sprays and chemicals used in agriculture. And the poison is sometimes passed on to the peregrine. It would be a thousand pities if the peregrine falcon, so long a part of the traditional fell country scene, was to disappear from our crags. Lovers of wild nature should do everything in their power to save him.

Simultaneously with the gradual disappearance of the peregrine there have been several reports of the golden eagle being seen over Lakeland. In some cases watchers might have seen buzzards, and not eagles, but it is fairly certain that the golden eagle has been in the district, probably flying south from known eyries in the south of Scotland in a search for possible nesting places. More than once I have seen eagles as far south as Ayrshire, and no doubt such a bird could easily fly to the Lake District, but the experts do not think he would stay long. Two hundred years ago—according to Lake District parish registers—you got a shilling for killing an eagle and the award for a fox was three shillings and fourpence. In spite of this encouragement to slaughter, foxes have continued to thrive, but the eagle, a creature of low fecundity, has gradually disappeared. Probably its end was hastened by the "long, strong rope" kept in Borrowdale in 1785 for the purpose of "letting men down into the rocks to take the nests and young of the eagles", and the great bird was finally driven out of the district about 160 years ago. The chances of his being able to find the necessary seclusion and food in the Lakeland of today seem very slim indeed and the possibility that they could breed successfully here again, extremely remote.

There is a quiet corner beyond the Brathay that is famed for its white-washed, story-book houses, its lush meadows, meandering streams and deep, cool woods, and even for its old-world hostelries and the excellence of their beer. Most of these charms have been captured on the picture postcards but I once discovered a new feature of this pleasant place which is perhaps not so photogenic—the skill of the menfolk at cooking, jam making, fruit bottling, and other crafts of the kitchen. Hawkshead show comes every September and among the crowds of country women in the big Home Industries tent you will also find courageous husbands and fathers—checking up on whether they have won prizes for orange marmalade or embroidery. And many of them have. One year, it was, for instance, a man who won the diploma awarded by a woman's journal for bottled fruit, and the men were equally prominent among the biscuits, squares of gingerbread, and "packed lunch for one, drinks included". Obviously, the onslaught by the men had been appreciated in advance that September for the organizers had thrown in a special class, "any cake made by a man (not iced)". Here the competition was keen and one had the feeling that the cake-makers could have tackled even iced cake with confidence. Clearly, the winner knew what he was doing for he also carried off the medal for the best exhibit in the cookery classes, but what the women thought about this I cannot say. But it was the "embroidery in wool" and "example of basketry" classes that put the tin hat on it, for here the only competitors were men, although, chivalrously, they made no challenge with "knitted socks".

The char fishers are often active on Windermere and Coniston Water and occasionally on one or two other lakes and tarns, during September. There seem to be more char fishers about these days and the char, they say, are getting bigger. A few years ago a char fisher could get six or seven shillings a pound for his fish, and a good char weighs about half a pound and is perhaps ten inches long. When I was a boy there would be eight of them to a pound. Perhaps there is an art in char fishing, or "trolling" as they call it round here, but it is not the mystery it used to be. It was said that the hooked "bait" had to be made of gold or at any rate covered in gold plate, but you can catch char with copper, silver, or almost any bright metal. But perhaps the best "bait" used to be made from the reflectors in old carriage lamps. There is no more succulent fish than the Lakeland char—more tasty even than fresh brown trout newly fried in butter.

A summer evening climb when workaday cares are over is possible if you live on the edge of the Lake District. Two of us reached our Langdale crag one September evening within an hour of the office, the one changing in the car while the other drove, and then turnabout. The crag gets the full glare of the evening sun and it was almost too hot in shirt sleeves. Not even a wisp of cloud in the blue sky and a feeling in the air that there'd be no rain for weeks. Difficult to realize it had been pouring down a day or two earlier and that this was the first sunny week of the summer. Far below us we could see the farmers getting in their month's late hay and we watched, between pitches, the new patterns being made by the rattling reapers in the harvest fields. Cars and coaches, like tiny toys, moved slowly along the valley and the evening peace was occasionally shattered by an explosive motor-cycle zigzagging up to Blea Tarn. Sheep nosed about in the brackens below the foot of the crag, but no other movement apart from an occasional lazy flicker of rope from another party on the far side of the crag. Much too hot to be energetic, we thought, so we sat and smoked between pitches, sighed for a sight or sound of running water and thought of long, cool draughts in some quiet, shadowed room. We watched the sun go down behind the purple hills, and the stillness of the evening had come upon the valley when we finished our climb, coiled the rope, and shuffled down the dusty screes and through the brackens to the road.

On another September day two of us looked down from the Scandale fells along a deep, green valley towards two lakes, a handful of tarns, and a distant, shining strip of sunlit sea. We were perhaps three miles away from the busy main road, but we had seen nobody all day except an old shepherd with two dogs at heel. The only sound was a faint murmuring of running becks, but there was a sense of urgent movement everywhere. The clouds were billowing like a Monday washing day, the cloud shadows chasing one another in gay abandon up and down the fells, the wind patterns on the distant water constantly changing, the bracken waving and rippling in the breeze, and the birds blown helter-skelter across the sky. With the whole of the southern part of the Lake District at our feet, and not even the sight of a distant motor-car or a strip of roadway to bring us down to earth, it was possible to attempt an appraisal of the scene, and to decide why this could only be our own corner of England and nowhere else. The reason, we felt, was simply the trees. In many parts of Britain there are mountains, lakes, and crags no less fine or rewarding, but nowhere else, we thought, are the tilted lands and quiet waters so richly scattered and ringed in forest, woodland and coppice. And it was strange to realize that down among the trees, in the hollows in the hummocked land, unseen and unheard, were hidden thousands of our fellows, their homes and their thousand cars, while all we could see were three grazing sheep, stolid and sturdy against the rising wind.

After the rock that has given us the shape of the hills and the valleys it is the things that grow—the vegetation, the woodlands, the flowers, the animals, and the birds—that mostly go to make up the Lake District. But while the rock—unless gouged out for reservoirs and roads—is with us for all time, the plant and animal life is never safe, and is indeed less safe now than ever before. Every day it is being destroyed, dug up, shot, stolen, poisoned, burned, or attacked in other ways so that while it is here today it may well be gone tomorrow. Many factors are contributing to the desecration and slaughter—the growing use of machinery and chemicals in agriculture, for instance, or the changing pattern of forestry, or the invasion of the motor-car, or even the "discovery" of the countryside by the masses—and if the Lake District as we used to know it is not to disappear altogether something must be done about it. Fortunately, however, there are still many people who care deeply about these things—people who believe that beautiful, natural and harmless things like trees and flowers or birds and insects are important—and within recent years a great deal of quiet work has been going on to preserve the things that live and grow in and around the fell country. Towards the end of 1962 all this devotion and effort culminated in the official inauguration of the Lake District Naturalists' Trust when, at last, a start began to be made to halt the molestation and make the area a safer place for wild life and the quiet things of nature.

Hardknott Fort on a wet September evening, Nearly two thousand years had passed since the Roman legionaries stood on the same spot and looked down along the green trough of Eskdale to the sea and northwards to the highest hills in England. Little had changed over the centuries—a little less woodland nowadays on the lower slopes perhaps, rather more bracken and the stone walls marching over the fells, but still the same shapes peeping through the clouds, the same winding track over the pass, the same tumbled, black crags, the ravines and the tremendous solitude. How many times, I wondered, as I stood inside the fort, shoulders hunched against the driving rain, had the Romans stood up there on just such another evening, watching the storm clouds gathering over Scafell and sadly thinking of their distant, sunny homeland? Four sodden Herdwicks, cropping the grass inside the fort, shared my vigil and now and again, one of them would shake itself in a cloud of spray. A pair of ravens wheeled high above the pass but the winding road was deserted and the only sound came from the flooded beck. Down to the left, below the muddied track, were the remains of the baths where the soldiers steamed and behind me was their exercise ground. The commandant's office was straight ahead and the four watch towers plain to see. That day, almost within sight of the world's first atomic power station, they were "restoring" this link with our early days, uncovering the old walls, putting each stone back in place. With so much ahead of us the past suddenly seemed important.

One of the most useless pieces of weather lore to have by you so far as the Lake District is concerned is the couplet that begins; "Red sky at night is the shepherd's delight . . ." As often as not the exact reverse is the truth, and this applies equally to the rest of the adage. Often in September you get good examples of the unreliability of this old saying—an incredibly shocking day following a magnificent golden sunset, or a bright, sunny day unexpectedly chasing an unusually vivid morning. All that you can do is to mistrust a red sky most heartily whether it occurs in the evening or the morning, so that occasionally you may get a pleasant surprise. "Too bright, too early" is often a fairly reasonable guide, while an exceptional sunset nearly always precedes a remarkable day. The unfortunate thing is that the day is just as likely to be remarkable for rain as for sunshine. Farmers are popularly supposed to be infallible weather prophets but they must never be relied upon outside their own few acres. To them a patch of mist or cloud on a distant top or the wind coming from behind a particular wood might be of great significance, but take them into the next parish and they're lost. They might sniff the air, or throw straws into the wind, or even put up a moistened finger, but they've really no more idea than you or me. And you've only got to listen to the B.B.C. forecasts to realize that the mountains make their own weather.

But I remember one wonderful September day in 1964 when the hills looked as sharp against the blue sky as if they had been cut out with scissors, when the smoke rose straight from the chimney pots in the valley, and you could almost hear the insects talking. I was alone on the Dodds, those little-visited hills to the north of the Helvellyn range, and not only saw nobody all day but hardly heard a sound either. Three miles away coachloads of tourists were noisily exploring Aira Force—I saw some of them on my way down—and I've no doubt there were processions going over Helvellyn, but nobody else had thought it worthwhile going up into these fells that look more blank on the map than any other part of the National Park, except perhaps the bleak country at the back of Skiddaw. True, there's nothing very exciting about the Dodds, for there are no crags except some down by the road, no tarns to speak of—just a couple of pools—almost no sculpturing of the mountain sides, little bracken and heather, just miles of grass. But in place of the normal attractions there are the loneliness, the quietude, the splendid turf that makes such easy going, and the feeling that you can look out, around the whole compass, at the bigger mountains, as if from some upland promenade. Perhaps people knew these hills better a hundred years ago, for last century coaches travelled an old road that contours round the fellside and the passengers would at least peer up the hillsides and maybe even knew who was the Mr. Watson of Watson's Dodd. And a thousand years earlier men were digging into one corner for lead. But today not many people go into these smoothly rounded hills.

10

AUTUMN PAGEANT
October

I CAN'T remember a more perfect October in Lakeland than that of 1965. Almost every day that month we awakened to still, hazy mornings that blazoned an hour or two later into days of glorious sunshine and unbroken blue skies. Morning after morning I watched the great red orb of the sun rise slowly from behind Benson Knott and gradually melt away the mists that cloaked the fells, until they emerged, first in hazy outline and then in sharp focus. Elsewhere in the country they had fog but not in Westmorland. The great winds that sometimes sweep the leaves from the trees within a day or two also spared us for most of the month, and instead, the gold and russet carpet kept on daintily falling, a little more each day, and the trees moved into autumn with grace and dignity. Never has there been a finer pageant of colour in the woods, along the roadsides and across the bracken-covered fellsides and often the lakes mirrored the scene to perfection. One day that month we came down off St. Sunday Crag and saw the length of Ullswater stretching out towards the distant meadows around Pooley Bridge, the lake shining in the late afternoon sunlight like a smooth scimitar curved around the flank of Place Fell, and its three tiny islands riding like toy yachts at anchor. Down through the steep woodlands, along a rustling carpet of leaves, we came, and, through a gap in the larches, looked across the Grisedale Beck at Lanty's Tarn on its little ledge above the lake. There's an old wood of ragged Scots firs beside the tarn and even from that distance we

could see the trees exactly mirrored in the tiny pool. Down in
the valley the dogs were barking at Grassthwaite How and the
rattling of pails came winging up the hillside but there were no
other sounds and the smoke from the cottage chimneys in Patterdale rose slowly straight to the sky.

It's a gradual process, this preparation for the long winter,
but the magical effect seems to come almost overnight. We
wake up some sunny morning, before the gales blow all the
leaves away, to discover that the picture has been repainted
while we slept from the other side of the palette—the warm
colours of brown, yellow, orange and red in place of the familiar green. There's a new smell of woodsmoke in the air from
the cottage fires and the weekend gardeners, and soon enter-
prising small boys will be hauling bonfire material across the
fields and along the lanes. There was a time when the fell
country went into its long winter sleep about this time of the
year—the last holidaymakers departed, the traffic stilled, the
hotels closed and the village streets deserted—but those days
are now gone. For the traffic remains, with a new purposeful
bustle everywhere, and a sunny weekend still brings out the
trippers in their thousands. The farmer, perhaps, with his fields
ploughed and his fences clipped back, can take things a little
easier, and the boatmen can get on with their painting, but the
forester will be busier than ever and most bright mornings
now the hunters will be away to the fells.

Over the low wall just ahead of my car one October morning
a red shadow slithered noiselessly in the bright morning sunlight and immediately disappeared in a larch wood above the
Troutbeck road. A moment later the exciting music of a pack
in full cry suddenly rang out clear, along streamed a jumble of
struggling white and brown shapes, and in a flash, a dozen
eager hounds had leapt the wall and crashed into the undergrowth. The music died away as the chase faded into the mist
hanging in the valley bottom, and I had moved off before either
the red-coated huntsman or his followers had arrived. I don't
know whether they pulled down this particular fox, but if he
did get away no doubt he'd be at the Christmas poultry before
long.

Once the clocks have been put back and the fell packs have
begun hunting in earnest we feel that winter's not far away.

The weekly newspapers start about this time giving their "Hunting Appointments" with times and places for those who want to join a hunt—or watch from the car as so many do nowadays. One newspaper publishes a picture of an opening meet—the master, the huntsman, and the whip, well booted for the fray, with sticks in one hand and glasses in the other, all ready to move off. With them are the hounds, sleek enough now and rid of their summer fat, and the little tousled terriers, with their sharp, beady eyes peeping through fierce, tufted brows. This particular huntsman has been at the game for forty years and has perhaps accounted for as many mountain foxes as any man in history. A short, stocky man in heavy boots, baggy breeches, old coat, and a short crop and lead in his hand. Very few people knew more about terriers than this quiet-spoken dalesman who can tell you the characteristics of each one of his hounds. He will spot a fox streaking into a distant borran before you or I could focus our eyes, and he knows these fells as well as some people know their back gardens. And until somebody can think of a better way to deal with foxes he and his kind will continue to perform a very useful service in these parts.

On the banks of the beck that tumbles down from Goats Water, and hardly distinguishable from the boulders that lie around, is a simple tombstone marking the grave of a gallant foxhound. Just a rough, rectangular piece of rock fallen from the crag above, but if you examine it closely you will be able to read in simple carving—"Charmer, 1911". Nearly everyone knows of the memorial stone on Helvellyn to the dog that spent many weeks, about 160 years ago, by the side of its dead master's body, but few people know of Charmer's grave. Wordsworth and Scott wrote poetry about the fidelity of poor little Foxey, but Charmer remains unsung. Charmer was just an ordinary Lake Country foxhound and she died doing her everyday job. One wintry day many years ago a hunted fox took refuge in Dow Crag, and Charmer, with other hounds of the Coniston pack, went in after it, but they never found the fox and had to be rescued later with ropes. It was dark when the hunt got down to the valley and when they had a count they found that Charmer was missing. She was never seen alive again. Some days later they heard her baying from the crag,

Scafell Pike and Scafell from Wastwater
Ennerdale; Pillar and the Rock on the left

but about the time dalesmen reached the foot, the hound, excited perhaps by the hope of rescue, missed her footing on a narrow ledge and fell 400 feet to the screes. She had perished because she had gone back into the crag alone, determined to reach her quarry. It was the dalesmen who buried her, carved her stone, and planted it above her grave.

Perhaps a mile or so away from Charmer's grave, and just a few feet away from the well-marked Walna Scar track is a rough circle of stones where, nearly four thousand years ago, people who lived on this lonely moor before the dawn of history, held strange rites and buried their dead. Few of the climbers who regularly pass this way know the spot, for it is only when you are standing in the very centre of the ring that you realize the significance of the stones. From the track they look just the same as the thousands of rocks that lie littered across the fellside. One October day I stood in the rain in the centre of the circle as I had often done before, trying to picture these people of the mist of so long ago and wondering what really happened in this desolate place between the mountains and the lake. The stones make as perfect a circle as you could draw with a stick and a long piece of string, there is nothing accidental about them, and, from the centre, you can detect openings north, south, east, and west. Human sacrifices? I don't know. But just over fifty years ago they dug up the place and discovered urns, a piece of charred woollen stuff, a clay bead, some human bones, and a tiny cup containing a baby's tooth. Perhaps the antiquarians can guess at the meaning of it all—a Bronze Age cemetery perhaps, or a sacred spot where the gods were appeased—but on a wet October day with the mists swirling across the fell it seemed important just to realize that it all happened before the days of Helen of Troy.

There are the first reminders about this time of the year of approaching Yuletide—perhaps a dusting of snow on Cross Fell, the "Christmas Club" notices in the shops and, already, the announcements of forthcoming Christmas whist drives. The prizes are always the same—turkeys, geese, ducks, chickens, and so on—so there's plenty of scope in the poultry runs for the foxes, if they can escape the hunts and the farmers with their shotguns. Time was when the turkeys and geese used to dis-

10

Strange rocks on Bowfell
Killington and the Howgills

appear after the whist drives in the large cars of expert players from the towns, but not now. Country folk seem to have discovered their own methods of hanging on to their Christmas dinners.

At this time of the year you will see the farmers reaping the October harvest of the fells—scything the bracken for winter bedding for the cattle. In a short time they seem to be able to the enough for half the beasts in Westmorland, but when the ueaped farm carts have rumbled off down the lane the only signs of their labours will be a few worn patches in the great carpet of russet and gold wrinkled over the fells. There seems no other use for bracken—apart from its scenic value—and whether for bedding or as a background for the colour photographer the fronds must be dead or dying. Perhaps there are few finer sights in Lakeland than the autumn sun glowing on mile after mile of the rich covering with a foregound frame of red, orange, and yellow leaves, but the sheep farmer only sees the bracken as his worst enemy. Every new acre means so much less grazing and each year the silent invader is creeping higher up the fellsides, spreading through the intake fields, or even marching boldly up to the farmhouse door. There has never been so much on the fells before and there is so little one can do about it in a tilted land. Farmers may hack or crush it, scientists rack their brains for new poisons, or you may spray it from the air, but even if you kill it for the time being the old enemy soon pops up again in a new place.

The worst bracken I ever encountered was some stuff nearly six feet high into which I once stumbled when coming down off Slioch in Wester Ross. It was, I remember, a wet day, and when we finally emerged from the thickets we felt as if we had just scrambled out of Loch Maree. There are any number of theories about how to control bracken. One is that if you can crush or bruise it once a year for three successive years it will lay down and die, although some people say you have to do the crushing three times in the same season. Scientists and Ministry of Agriculture specialists have even tried to encourage disease in bracken so that it will kill itself off, but the experiments were stopped when it was found the the plants were thriving on the injected viruses. Everything has been tried—selective weed killers, spraying from the air, ferocious-looking crushing machines—but unless a miracle happens, the brackens—the dalesman uses the plural word—are here to stay.

Experts tell me it is the acid in the soil that encourages the brackens, and that regular liming of the fellsides would perform the twofold blessing of reducing the growth and helping the sheep with their calcium deficiency. But how on earth do you lime all these thousands of tilted acres? The only way would be from the air, and this seems at present to be both impracticable and expensive. Spraying from the air is all very well when you are dealing with flat fields in an open countryside, but there are a hundred and one difficulties and dangers when you try to do it in the mountains. Unless the weather—and, in particular, the wind—is just right, the operation just can't be done satisfactorily with present-day equipment, although I dare say helicopters, properly adapted for the job, might be worth persevering with. I know one Lake District farmer who, tired of waiting for suitable flying conditions, went off on his own up the fellside with a spraying machine fastened to his back. All he got for his trouble was backache, and, in a few weeks' time, a slight withering of the brackens in one tiny corner. By the following year, however, the brackens had fully recovered from the shock and were sprouting more vigorously than ever. And crushing machines fall down, of course, because you can't use them on steep fellsides, really steep fellsides, any better than you can use a tractor. For in addition to the slope there are the hidden boulders and rocks. A £1,000 machine could be wrecked in a week.

Bracken is rarely found above the 2,000-feet contour and most of it is below 1,500 feet, but this means that even on the highest Lake District mountains only the top thousand feet or so are relatively free. Heather seems to grow at any height in Lakeland, but often where it has been burned to allow the grass to sprout it is the bracken that is coming through instead.

Apart from choking the grass and herbs the brackens can also be poisonous to sheep. They sometimes eat the young shoots, particularly after they have gone back from the intakes to the fells, and the young cattle, too, sometimes develop a taste for the fronds. The poison, I am told, can kill them in time, but, apart from this danger, there is the ever-present chance that the animals will come to prefer bracken to their proper feed and suffer accordingly. Cattle that have eaten bracken have sometimes to be kept in the byre for several days and dosed with linseed oil. I have read somewhere that many years ago Germany used to import brackens from Australia of all places and extract from them some substance that went into the making of explosives, which suggests that there is more in bracken than merely the colourful carpet we so often admire. Throughout almost the whole year—spring, perhaps, excepted —the bracken carpet looks well on the fells. In summer, as the fronds are uncurling, the fells are clothed in pale larch green but when the autumn comes the colours gradually change into bronze, red, gold and yellow, with perhaps other colours in between, and one's fingers itch for a colour camera.

Go into the woods around the foothills of Wetherlam any October day, even a dull, damp day, and you will find all the colours in the world. Could there be anywhere with more varieties of trees in so small a space? They are all there by choice, still bursting with life and packed so closely you can hardly squeeze through, while the remains of the conifers planted sixty years ago at the bleak head of the ravine are all either dead, black sticks or scraggy, storm-blown stragglers. Down in the woods are slender birches with their leaves shining like golden sovereigns, graceful larches hung with tapestry foliage, their uptilted fingers trembling in the breeze, well-berried rowans, oaks, alders, willows, blackthorns, and, propping the dry-stone wall, a noble old yew. In the ravine the trees hang confidently over the water from the sketchiest of root hold, bestriding waterfalls with grace and abandon, while through the thick carpet of leaves the baby trees are sprouting, thick as spring snowdrops. Right to the very edge of the great quarry hole crowd the trees, and if you peer over you will even see the birches sprouting from cracks in the dark green, vertical walls, recklessly alive on handfuls of windblown soil. An old tawny owl lives in the damp darkness of the lower quarry, and on my last visit we crept on tiptoe through the rustling leaves to see if we could spot him. Not a sign of him at first, and then, on the snapping of a twig, a great brown shape came winging noiselessly across the gloomy pit and swept up into the trees.

At one time, the woodlands of Lakeland choked the valleys

and marched some distance up the fells. Perhaps the area has fewer trees now—despite the tens of thousands planted by the Forestry Commission—than at any time in its history, but to-day, at least, there is no indiscriminate slaughter and the felling is controlled. Once the area even had its great forests—Ingle-wood, Copeland and Allerdale, for instance—and some of them might have been among the biggest in the country. The wild boar and the deer, red and fallow, roamed these woodlands and there were laws for the protection of the game and, no doubt, poachers and outlaws. But long ago these ancient forests dis-appeared and today Lakeland is a countryside of woodlands and copses scattered through the valleys and across the foot-hills. And it is these scattered woodlands that give Lakeland its infinite variety and much of its intimate atmosphere.

So much of this beauty is man made—unconsciously so, per-haps—but we tend to take it all for granted. Many of the trees are indigenous but many have been imported, although they are now accepted as natives. The larch is one of these—an especially lovely tree of the lower fells, although Wordsworth thought it would do considerable damage to the appearance of the countryside. The spring green of the larch in its perfect setting against the dark shadows of ravines or the grey crags is one of the sights of Lakeland, and, in the wintertime, one can admire these sturdy trees bent against the wind on an exposed ridge or flicking the snow from their uplifted fingers.

Perhaps in years to come we may feel the same affection for another foreigner—the Sitka spruce—which has come in for a great deal of harsh criticism. Planted as a commercial crop in straight lines, the spruce can offend against one's feeling for the casually natural, but it is surprising what time and good forestry can do to remedy the scar. The Thirlmere conifers, for instance, are now taking a most pleasing pattern and it may not be long before guide-book writers are commending the beauty of these man-made forests instead of condemning them.

One of the oldest of the Lakeland trees is the birch—the tree that gives valleys like Borrowdale and Dunnerdale their particular grace. The delicate tracery of its leaves against the sky can be a delight, but especially I admire the silver of its straight trunk. Seen against the dark green of the Scots firs, as in the Cairngorms, the birch makes the perfect frame to a mountain scene and it can also ideally break up the outline of a country house.

In my part of Westmorland, the ash is perhaps the commonest tree and I can pick inch-high seedlings out of my borders, blown or carried by birds, any springtime. Further up the fell-sides there is the rowan, weighed down in October with its berries, and also the juniper, while among the limestone stands the yew, dark and brooding against the white rock. And, along the lanes, the thorns and the hazels and the wild cherry, with, here and there, the chestnut, the oak and the beech. Those who believe in the significance of the autumn crop of berries expect a hard winter when the hedges are full of new splashes of scarlet. On the other hand, there is also the old saying that ice on the ponds before Martinmas—"thick enough to bear a duck"—foretells a mild winter, and October often brings the first morning hoar frost and even, at times, a flurry of snow on the hills. But the sensible will avoid trying to forecast the winter weather, especially after recent topsy-turvy years.

An old pack-horse track zigzagging up into the Coniston fells is being used for bringing down the slate from one of Lakeland's newer quarries. Actually, it is a disused quarry that has been reopened, and this is the pattern of development nowa-days in our second traditional local industry. But people have grumbled about the new scar on a mountainside which, for centuries, has been pockmarked with tunnels, shafts, holes, caves, and spoil heaps. These signs of man's enterprise, they say, are ugly and out of place. But why be ashamed of an ancient local craft, particularly one associated with the rock that gives Lakeland its very shape and beauty? Here, in days when the young people from the dales tend to leave the district because of lack of opportunities, is a fine worthwhile industry that long ago established Lakeland slate as the finest in the world. The slate quarries of Lakeland do not mean smoking chimneys, blackened buildings, and hurrying crowds, but rather a few huts roughly built from the stone so readily at hand, steep tracks metalled from the slate, spoil heaps of the same lovely material, green, blue, or grey, perhaps an aerial rope-way here and there, and the whirr of the diamond saw.

Scattered about Lakeland are several old, disused workings,

some of them overhung with trees, patterned with brambles, or flecked with lichen and flowers. Even the highest deserted quarries with their great vaulted chambers, their fern-decked tunnels, their man-made scree slopes, and their tumbledown stone huts, are interesting places rather than eyesores—places where you can watch Nature gradually reclaiming her own. The newly exposed rock may look a little raw for a time, but Nature will soon heal these places just as she does each year after the ice has split the crags. We must not be ashamed of our rock, nor of our honest local toil. And there's not much difference between a spoil-heap and a scree-slope. It's all the same wonderful stone.

The snow was lying several feet deep at the top of the gullies dropping into Deepdale from the summit of Fairfield towards the end of October 1962—the first snows of the winter and one of the earliest Lakeland falls I can remember. From the valleys all you could see was a light sprinkling of snow on the tops but if you went to the right places you could plunge up to your knees in the stuff—and even deeper. Fairfield, for instance, appeared to carry no more than a dusting on its top 300 feet above Rydal Head but, in fact, there were the beginnings of cornices up there and you could even have slid about a bit on skis.

Near the top of one of the snow-filled gullies we found a young ewe hopelessly marooned by the steepness of the snow above and the rather frightening looking crags below. She had got into the gully from the side—we could see her hoof-prints in the snow—and had then spent several hours, judging from the hundreds of tiny prints, trying to climb the cornice. But as the top six feet or so of the cornice were quite vertical this was impossible. When we saw her she was lying on her back, exhausted and no doubt patiently awaiting her end.

One of us kicked steps down the cornice and got the sheep on to its feet, but despite all our efforts we failed to drag or cajole her out of the side of the gully and more than once she slithered down towards the crags. If we had had a rope the rescue would have been a comparatively simple matter, but we were only on a simple Sunday afternoon walk. Carrying her might have been feasible with an ice axe for support, but, completely unsecured as we were, it seemed foolhardy to throw caution to the winds in such a steep place, and several times we nearly lost her over the edge. So in the end we left her in the gully, looking rather forlorn but safer than we had found her. We felt rather ashamed of ourselves, but decided she would probably come to less harm if left alone than if we had persisted in our rescue bid. The snows wouldn't last for long and perhaps she might eventually be able to work her way out at the side. She was starting to nuzzle her way through the snow to the grass when we left. At least she was sheltered from the biting wind and safe enough for a day or two if she restricted her explorations. This October snow was early enough to have caught out both the shepherds and the sheep. This young ewe was probably spending her first winter on the fells, and had perhaps never met snow this deep before. Snow, hail, gales and freezing cold at the end of one of the best Octobers in memory were hardly to be expected.

But my diary tells of many different October days. One of them two of us sat smoking in a bilberry-carpeted corner high up on Dow Crag. The sun lit up the steep sweep of precipice below our feet and glowed on the craggy side of the Old Man across the corrie, but most of the tarn nearly a thousand feet below, lay black and forbidding in the shadows. Tiny figures, looking like matches, appeared for a moment or two at the distant cairn—insignificant dots in a wild, soaring landscape. A bubble of laughter, caught by a rising zephyr, came winging up from the coloured specks of the tarn, and a quick, white flash in the one sunlit corner told of a mid-October bathe. A raven shot out of the crag like a whirling clay pigeon and then— for the fun of it—rolled and looped over the combe, and a four-engined plane, a minute silver dart in the sunlight, moved slowly across the blue zenith. Four hundred feet below our perch lay my dog, a tiny splash of black and white in a rocky, grey-brown world. So long as he could see us, swarming up the rock wall, he would lie content, musing on our stupid antics. Soon—for he could not see this far—he might set off to search for us, but a whistle or a shouted command would reassure him and he would lie down again to await our return with stolid resignation . . . A summer haze lay over the distant, sleepy landscape, and little winged insects whirred in the dry grass. Winter seemed very far away.

On another October day—the first day of "winter time"—I was sitting in my shirt sleeves on the top of Bowfell. It was very warm, sunny, almost cloudless, with very little wind and with that remarkable clarity in the atmosphere that you rarely see in the holiday months. From the summit, an hour before sunset, the Cumberland coast and the Solway Firth appeared very close at hand, and the shape of Criffel in Scotland, nearly forty miles away as the crow flies, was very distinct. Of course, there was nothing remarkable in this. I have seen and photographed the Outer Hebrides from the Cuillin Hills in Skye, more than sixty miles away, and the Isle of Man is a common enough sight, on clear days, from many places along the Furness and Cumberland coasts. And it is even possible, occasionally, to catch a glimpse of the Irish hills as I have done from Scafell more than once.

But sometimes in October you can meet fierce weather on the tops with winds so strong you could almost lean on the gusts, and flurries of hail whipped into your face like gravel thrown against a wall. On these days gulls and smaller birds get flung across the sky like blown leaves, and even the patient Herdwicks, heads into the gale and fleeces windswept, seem insecure as they slowly battle along their tiny "trods". Sometimes it is pouring down—great, grey curtains of rain sweeping majestically across the shadowed fells—and the only view the steep, tussocky, rock-strewn slope ahead. But these are just the sort of days when you may well get your reward, even though it is only a sudden patch of blue through a gap in the storm-wracked sky, a pale gleam of sunlight on the ferns around a waterfall, and a quick glimpse, before the clouds close in again, of white horses on a deserted beach far below and the distant, surging sea. But it will be enough and afterwards before a blazing fire with a bath and a good meal behind you the discomforts of two hours earlier are forgotten.

You can sometimes see them bringing down the Herdwicks off the fell in October—a few hundred grey-faced mothers and their black-faced lambs. A few hours later the mothers, less the draught ewes destined for the autumn sales, are back on their "heaf" while the the lambs are down in the in-by fields. From now on the lambs are on their own. They will never see their mothers again unless by chance at the dipping when mutual recognition is unlikely. The gathering is an ordinary sort of job for the shepherds, but to the town dweller it can smack of magic. Six sheepdogs handled one round-up I watched, with the casual assistance of three shepherds. Within two or three hours they discovered every sheep on a long, high stretch of rocky fellside and chivvied them all down through the intake fields to the farm. While the shepherds worked slowly down and across the fell occasionally giving a whistle or a shout, the dogs scurried through the bracken and scree, up and down the mountain, along rocky ledges, and in and out of steep ravines. Towards the end of the round-up a shepherd spotted three sheep, missed by the drive, contentedly grazing below a water-fall. One sharp whistle to a dog high up on the fellside and a point with his sharp crook was all that was required. In a few moments the sheepdog, out of sight of the sheep, had found them, winkled them out of the gill, and had them streaming across the fell towards their fellows.

It was dark enough for sidelights as I drove one October evening through Ambleside on my way to Wasdale over the passes, but a little further on there was the last golden glow of the sunset lighting up the black nick in the skyline at the top of Wrynose. Ten minutes later it was quite dark, so that the Three Shire Stone seemed suddenly to rear out of the night like a great finger warning me of the unseen drop below. There was no other vehicle going over the passes and the only light the tiny glimmer of a farmhouse far down in Dunnerdale. But plenty of life about. Every now and again a rabbit, caught in the beam of my headlights, would scatter, helter-skelter, down —or up—the road until he got tired, when he would suddenly dart over the edge or scamper up the fellside into the blackness. But the sheep, sturdy grey-faced Herdwicks, their eyes agleam in the headlights, showed no fear of the night intruder, but remained sprawled in the middle of the road, patiently awaiting the next move with not even surprise showing on their sad, resigned faces. Sometimes they would slowly drag themselves to their feet, and trot to the side of the track, but, as often as not, they preferred to wait until I gently nudged them with my bumper. Once or twice I had to get out to push them away. Had they been asleep already? But why in the middle of the road? It was just the same on Hardknott and, of course, they had selected their beds exactly on the steepest and sharpest corners. Three hours later I drove back over the silent passes, fitfully lit this time by a cloud-dodging moon, and the sheep were still there—fast asleep, most of them, I thought. It took me a long time to get home.

The only other people on Grey Crag in Birkness Combe one wet and misty October morning in 1965—and, so far as we knew, on this side of the fells—were two elderly gentlemen with an old rope and wearing old-fashioned climbing rig. On our way up to the crag we had met their companion—an even older man—picking his way down the screes through mist and drizzle, wet through and perspiring, but apparently enjoying himself, "I just came up for the walk," he explained as we chatted in the rain with the swollen beck swirling past our feet. "I'm too old to climb now." Ten minutes later and a few hundred feet higher up in the mist we came upon his friends, just off their climb and on their way down for hot baths and food. We recognized the leader, a distinguished scholar then seventy-seven years of age, and we guessed the old gentleman on the screes must have been over eighty. Fifty-three years before—you can see it in the records—the leader had made the very first route on this crag, and he had been back that morning with his friends, to do it again, in spite of the mist and rain and slimy rocks. There was no view—just swirling mists all round, the persistent drizzle, a noise of tumbling waters far below, and the great rocks, dark and greasy, rearing up towards the unseen sky. "I've always loved this place," said the leader as he shouldered his old rope and set off slowly down the steep, sliding screes. We had thought conditions too bad for climbing but now, for shame's sake, decided we must at least repeat their climb. If the weather was good enough for these old pioneers it should be good enough for us.

The leader was Sir Claude Elliott, the former headmaster of Eton College and once president of the Alpine Club, and his two companions were also distinguished mountaineers. I had met him years before when, well into the autumn of his days, he first came to retire to a lovely house beside the waters of Buttermere and within the shadow of the fells he knew so well.

Every morning, in old tweeds and battered hat, he would stroll down to the farm for milk, and although he had known this valley since he was a boy, and indeed, owned many of its pleasant acres, its changing beauty still fascinated him. Every few yards he must stop to peer in new wonder at the glint of the morning sunlight on a high shoulder of fell, watching the cloud shadows chasing through bracken, or study again how the screes changed colour after the rain. One September morning, as we sat chatting on the bridge, the air was filled with the "baa-ing" of hundreds of sheep brought down for the clipping, the barking of the farm dogs, the shouted orders of the shepherds, and the clatter of pails in the dairy. Some climbers passed through the fields on their way to the crags far above the valley, and I persuaded him to talk of those days, many years earlier, when he had pioneered some of the earliest climbs up there. I asked him, as he went back in memory over the years, how he used to manage a certain nasty little chimney, and, closing his eyes, he told me in detail, remembering, a lifetime afterwards, every move. And so it was pleasant to find him, years later, still climbing the crags of his youth, and seeking them out on a day that would have discouraged many people half his age. For people like this the hills are always worth while, no matter what the weather.

11

THE FIRST SNOWS
November

THE first snows usually come to the fells in November. You wake up some bright, crisp autumn morning and there's the snow, high up against a blue sky, and looking for all the world like icing sugar on a Christmas cake. And suddenly you feel energetic and refreshed and wonder whether it's time to overhaul the skis in the cellar. But next day the tops may be hidden in cloud and you can only guess whether or not the snow's still there, although sometimes the mists may lift for half an hour to reveal a white ridge line gleaming bravely in watery sunlight. And then it all melts away in a mild November drizzle, and all the glamour seems to go out of the sky. The old men in the dales grumble that we're in for a hard winter after heavy November falls, although early snows are often followed by a mild January or February. Nobody really knows. But these first snows of the winter bring a touch of magic to the Lake District scene, for there's nothing in the spring or summer or autumn glories of the fells to exceed the lonely, almost unearthly, beauty of white sunlit mountains.

November in the dales can be a jolly month—a month when the work in the fields is over and the farmer can get away to the hunting, the month of the shepherds' meets. The Lakeland fell sheep—particularly the Herdwick—is traditionally supposed to keep to its own heaf, but even so, a few hundred of them manage to roam far from home each year. And apparently they've always had this tendency to wander, for shepherds' meets, where the strays are exchanged, have been going on for much longer than the history books. The Troutbeck meet used to take place on the windswept summit plateau of High Street, 2,500 feet above sea-level, and one of the attractions, they say, was horse racing along the Roman "road". No doubt they used the same horses for dragging up the barrels of beer. But at the beginning of the century, perhaps after a succession of wild, wet meets high up in the clouds, they brought their headquarters 1,000 feet down the fellside to the bleak summit of Kirkstone Pass where at any rate there was a bit of shelter. It must have been easier to get the beer up there, too. Then, fifty years ago, human nature being what it is, they came down another 1,000 feet to a comfortable inn just above Troutbeck village and there are no signs yet of further removal.

A couple of days later there's the famous Mardale shepherds' meet, but it's a quiet affair nowadays compared with the days before the flooding of Mardale Green when the merrymaking used to go on from the Friday night until the following Wednesday. And throughout most of these five or six days the tough dalesmen were pouring ale down their throats as hard as they could. Nowadays this meet is held well away from the high fells and the sheep arrive by lorry instead of on foot over the passes. In the old days the festivities took place in the old Dun Bull, with its pleasant low rooms and clean, whitewashed walls, and the theme of the meet, as always, was the hunt. It was said that after a heavy night the great Joe Bowman could sing twenty verses of a hunting song at three o'clock in the morning and be out with his hounds before eight, fresh as paint. And each year they sing the grand old hunting chorus "Joe Bowman" to his memory, for Westmorland folk don't easily forget a man's man.

"Hunty" Bowman was born in 1850 and was made huntsman of the Ullswater pack in 1879. And, with the exception of four years, when George Salkeld took over, he hunted the pack until 1924. He was a man of fine physique and loved nature, children and all animals, so that the fox always got fair play. Joe upheld the best traditions of sportsmanship and they say that the "Mardale Hunt" and "Joe Bowman" were sung in army canteens all over the world in both great wars. One of the many stories of "Hunty" is that once, after a long hunt, he reached the Howtown landing stage intending to get back home on the lake steamer, but the officials demanded a ticket for each hound. Joe refused to pay but went on board leaving his hounds on the pier. But, when the steamer was half way across the lake to Glenridding Joe pulled out his horn and blew a resounding blast, whereupon the hounds, as if in full view of the fox, rattled along the path by the lake shore and were waiting at the pier in time to meet their master when he disembarked. It must have been a grand sight. Joe was buried in Patterdale churchyard in 1940 when his hunting horn was sounded for the last time.

Caldbeck where John Peel used to hunt, Eskdale, and other centres also have their shepherds' "merry neets", the business of exchanging stray sheep being a little more than an excuse nowadays for a good hunt in the fells and then a jovial evening with the old hunting choruses. These meets used to be quite exclusive, little affairs in their own way but nowadays sportsmen from far afield as well as holiday visitors by the score join in. The meal is always "tatie pot", mutton and potatoes, with plenty of pickles and apple pie and cheese to follow, and then a chairman is appointed and the serious business of the evening begins. The tray goes round and, as like as not, you'll have to sing for your supper. All the hunting choruses are sung over and over again, the huntsmen joining in with wild hoots on the horn. It is at occasions like these that one can catch the real flavour of Lakeland.

Meanwhile the strays wait patiently in their crowded pen, all safely identified by the old shepherd in charge. There will be a tattered old shepherds' book which lists the various markings, but probably the old shepherd and his assistant will be able to recognize the different sheep as accurately as you or I spot our friends. He can read the "pop" marks on the side of the sheep, the "lug" marks and the horn burns and decide at once to which flock the animal belongs. Each farm inherits its own earmarks— a practice which is said to have been handed down since the Vikings. If the ear is "cropped", according to the shepherds' guide, it means the end is chopped clean off, but it may also be "forked" or "bitted" which means slit down the centre. If they are "fork bitted" it means a V-shaped notch is cut out of the side of the ear, while "key bitted" means a square-cut notch. Each ear has a "top" side and a "bottom" side and the number of possible combinations is considerable. A description like this in the shepherds' guide may now perhaps be understood: "Cropped and under key bitted near, under halfed far, stroke from shoulder blade on near side, pop on tailhead." The "pops" are the round blobs, in different colours, often seen on a sheep's side. Sometimes there are stripes instead. And it is information like this that the average shepherd carries about with him in his head just as other people might remember telephone numbers

These old meets are often among the highlights of a shepherd's year. Conversation throughout is almost entirely confined to hunting or sheep—the first, a sort of dalemen's religion, and the second their livelihood. While the average person can exhaust his knowledge and interest in sheep in two or three sentences the shepherd can go on about them all night if necessary. A shepherds' meet can be a rollicking success even if the mist is so thick on the tops that the hunters, struggling against driving rain, hardly ever see the hounds, let alone a fox. Down in the inn, with a great fire roaring up the chimney and yesterday's trophy—a fine dog fox—hanging from the beams outside, it can be very pleasant if a trifle noisy. The shepherd's only bit of business is to stroll round to the sheep pen at the back and see if any of the assorted Herdwicks, Swaledales, and Roughs belong to him. The tightly packed sheep, so close that you could hardly put a stick between them, make neither sound nor movement, but the uncomplaining mass steams like a rugger pack on a clammy day. Nearly half may be Herdwicks, grey-faced and kindly of eye, and the remainder with black faces, shaggier coats, and a slighter fiercer look, mostly Swaledates. Almost undistinguishable from the latter, but with rather heavier fleeces, will be the straggly Roughs. Identification will be a moment's job. With the hunters returned, wet through and clamouring for refreshment, the real business of the meet can begin, and soon some old character will be leading the company through the fifteenth chorus of "The Mardale Hunt". The dalesman has a ready capacity for turning business into pleasure at the least provocation, and lost sheep have always been as good an excuse as any.

Long years ago the highest honour the Lakeland dalesfolk in some areas could confer on one of themselves was to appoint him the "mayor" of the valley, but unfortunately the custom

An island on Ullswater

gradually died out. Unlike our busy civic chiefs these country "mayors" had only one serious duty during their year of office— the arranging of the annual "Mayor Hunt", which was really just another good excuse for a "reet good do". It was just as well if the "mayor" knew something about hunting for he had to choose the line hounds should take, but this was not very vital. All that really mattered was that he had to be a person "of some substance"—perhaps the owner of a few dozen sheep —and, most important, he had to be the sort of chap who could lead a sing-song and get order when he wanted it. These were lively occasions, so it was pleasant to see the custom revived at Troutbeck about a dozen years ago, and it has continued ever since. They generally have a fox hunt, a meet of the beagles and perhaps some clay pigeon shooting, but the really serious business starts with the dinner, with drinks on the "mayor" for the last hour. At nine o'clock the name of the new "mayor" is announced, his name having been kept as close a secret as it is possible to keep one in Troutbeck, and until a late hour the hunting choruses echo round the room just as they did two hundred years ago.

In November 1963, Adam Slee an active old dalesman living near Windermere celebrated his hundredth birthday. His father, the legendary Lanty Slee, born in 1802—just three years out of the eighteenth century—was perhaps the only genuine Lake District smuggler who stands any chance of going down in history. For many years Lanty distilled a potent whisky in a variety of stills hidden about the district, and sold it to the more discerning gentry. But much more of it went over the old smugglers' road across the passes and down to the port of Ravenglass, where there was more than a passing interest in "the trade". The whisky went in bottles or bladders packed in panniers on the backs of ponies, led over the passes at the dead of night. Sometimes, they say, the hooves of the ponies trotting through the dark were bound in straw, the better to escape the excisemen, and occasionally there would be fights and scuffles in the mist, with a few broken heads and no questions asked in the morning. In one of Lanty's hideouts he had his "worm" hidden under the flags of the kitchen with a long pipe, cunningly contrived, carrying exhaust steam into a hedge in an adjoining field. Another den was in an old quarry, high up in the fells. It

11

Lanty's Tarn, Patterdale

was very good whisky, they say, but he asked only ten shillings a gallon for it. Of course, you had to know the ropes, and the correct gambit was to enquire whether he'd had a good crop of "taties" that year. After that he might be ready to talk business. But his son—he died in 1964—didn't remember much about this for most of it happened before he was born.

One November afternoon we reached one of Lanty's hideouts by slithering down to the foot of a deserted quarry a thousand feet above the Brathay, swarming up to the rough entrance hole and dropping ten feet into the darkness. This was where he made his whisky and we could see where he placed his "worm", and the pipe that carried the exhaust steam into the water tank, while the ashes of his last fire—lit more than a century before —were still undisturbed. There were the ashes of a hundred previous fires and, if you used your torch, you could see the rusted remains of old barrel hoops, and, underneath the stones at the back of the cave, the airy store for the brimming kegs. They say the excisemen never discovered this hide-out although they passed scores of times along the ancient smugglers' road of Wrynose Pass that you can see from the cave winding through the fells down to the sea.

The last time I saw Mr. George D. Abraham, the pioneer climber and photographer who died in 1965, was in November of the previous year. He was then ninety-three years of age and as we chatted, he sat contentedly, surrounded by his mountain pictures and his memories, in his Keswick home that looked out over one of the finest views in England. He was the last link with the deerstalker and Norfolk jacket pioneers who founded the sport of mountaineering in this country and, with his brother, the man who first popularized the sport with his photographs and his writings. For not only did he take his heavy plate camera into desperate places to picture determined-looking men hanging on to rocks by their eyebrows, but he also found new ways up vertical crags in Scotland and Wales as well as in his native Cumberland. And there was even a jagged aiguille high above Chamonix that used to bear his name. Remarkably, his memories of adventurous days fifty, sixty, and seventy years before were almost as sharp as the wonderful photographs that lined the walls of his home. He even remembered his very first climb—Pillar Rock by the old Slab and Notch route with the help of his mother's clothes line. "There were some Alpine Club men on the Rock that day," he recalls, "and they were very kind and helpful and didn't laugh at our silly rope. I thought, 'What wonderful men!' and decided to become a climber."

In 1892 George led his brother Ashley on the first ascent of Walla Crag Gully, the first climb ever done in Borrowdale. To get into the lower chimney he used for a foothold the exposed, withered root of an ancient holly tree, projecting, fed by some hidden soil, out of the vertical rock. As his weight came on the twist of dying fibre it sagged but did not snap and he was able to reach his holds above. Some years ago I happened to repeat the old climb and, like everyone before me, used the same old root, now scratched down to finger thickness. A few days later I was chatting to the old pioneer himself, and his first question was, "Is the old root still there?" How pleasant to be able to tell him that it was, that it still creaked ominously, but that it had withstood something like seventy years of use, and seemed likely to remain there for ever. I remember the old man, thinking back over a lifetime's memories, asked whether we had noticed the old track underneath the crags where once as boys they had found old coins, perhaps dropped by smugglers creeping by night across the steep fellside. He was still climbing at seventy, but in his later years could only lift his eyes to the hills that had been his whole life. And when he died there was nobody alive who could remember the earliest days when men first discovered the attraction of steep rocks.

In the attic of a house in the village of Coniston Mr. Bert Smith is hard at work from dawn till night making violins. Through his tiny roof window he can see a line of crags and above them the sky, but he has no time to look at the scenery for he has so much work to do. He is up at six o'clock, summer and winter, weekdays, and Sundays, and never puts down his tools before ten o'clock at night. Every year he makes four violins, fashioning each part, except the strings, with his own hands. Even his tools he made himself, and he scorns the use of machinery. You can buy violins made in a factory, the wood bent by steam, but the instruments made by this Lakeland craftsman are not ordinary violins. Each one is an exact copy of the great Italian masters, with the curves carved and not bent, and many famous violinists have told him what remarkably fine copies they are. Even the great Yehudi Menuhin has praised his work. I asked him the obvious question, "How do you get this wonderful tone?" and I got the obvious reply; "That's my secret." But he was prepared to tell me part of the story. Most of the secret, it seems, is in the varnishing—at least a six months' job—and the rest is in the tuning of the back of the violin. And so, for hours at a time, Mr. Smith is tapping away at thin pieces of wood, listening to the sound, taking off a shaving, and listening again. A craftsman certainly, but I suggest, an artist as well. And he seems to have only one relaxation—playing the violin. Who knows?—perhaps one day a "Bert Smith" will be as greatly praised as a "Stradivarius".

They sent a young Fell pony from the Westmorland hills to the Royal stud at Balmoral in November 1963 at the request, it is stated, of the Queen. It was George V who first introduced Fell ponies to Balmoral, and now, I'm told, they fit easily into the Highland scene. They are much bigger than Shetlands, something like thirteen to fourteen hands high, and probably originated from over the Border. They say the first Fell pony to be given a proper name was found, with trailing rein, cropping heather on the slopes of Stainmore after the remnants of the '45 had straggled through Westmorland. Whether he had been ridden by Scot or Englishman nobody knew, but they took him down to one of the farms and, for want of a better name, called him "Ling Cropper". And the same name persists throughout the breed to this day.

The game, scruffy-looking, little Lakeland terrier, sometimes in the news at this time of the year when lost for days in a fox's borran, is not the same animal as the Lakeland terrier winning prizes at Cruft's. The show dog, deep chested with thick, short legs and very like a miniature Airedale, is a handsome enough specimen, but, in the words of one Lakeland Master of Foxhounds, would make a fox die of fright—or laughter. Hunting folk will tell you that all the sporting ability has been bred out of him, and it is true that his short legs and bulky girth would make him useless for work in a fox-hole. But for all that he is registered at the Kennel Club as a separate breed and there must be hundreds of people who believe that these show champions are the dogs whose underground adventures keep hitting the headlines. The genuine working Lakeland terrier, on the other hand, has no real pedigree and the only time he is on show is at Lakeland sporting events where a torn ear or badly scratched face and paws do not lessen his chance of a prize. The only qualification for entry at these shows is that he should have worked for at least a season with a Lakeland pack. It does not matter whether he is black and grey, black and tan, all black, or even blue (which sometimes happens), so long as he is approximately the right shape and has plenty of guts. Most of all when he is hunting it is his courage and determination that count, and no dog has a bigger share of these qualities than the real, little Lakeland.

There are some November days when the whole of Lakeland is bathed in sunlight but the ten-mile trough of the largest lake in England completely filled with fog. From above the effect is remarkable—blue skies and sunshine all around but the valley shrouded in off-white cotton-wool, with here and there the tip of a mast just peeping through. Down in the fog one November the Windermere ferry was having its most exciting week for years. The ferry which hauls itself across the lake on chains was being overhauled, and passengers had to be taken across the 600 yards of water in an ordinary motor-launch. Several times it got itself lost—once it nearly ran aground on Belle Isle—and there were delays of up to an hour with the ferry going round in circles until somebody thought of taking a compass on board. There has been a ferry across the lake for hundreds of years and, down the centuries, excitements and tragedies galore, but the greatest disaster of all occurred on October 19th 1635 when forty-seven passengers, most of them members of a wedding party, together with their horses and carriages, were drowned. Ever since then, they say, the place, particularly the Lancashire side, has been haunted and you can still hear tales around Sawrey way of mysterious lights, weird cries in the night, and ghostly faces.

But some Novembers it rains hard in Lakeland. There was a

wet month, for instance, in 1958, but this was nothing to what it must have been like nearly seventy years ago. For example, they say that on Wednesday, November 2nd 1898, when the floods were at their height, it was possible—if you didn't mind getting drenched to the skin—to row right across Belle Isle on Windermere. The island was almost completely submerged, only the tree tops showing above the water. And they say the craft in the boathouses around Bowness Bay rose on the flooded lake waters until they were bobbing up against the ceilings. Kentmere reservoir was filled to the brim and there were fears that the dam might burst, while the Ambleside postman on his way to Dungeon Ghyll could get no further than Chapel Stile as the whole valley had become one huge lake. Bridges were destroyed, a train was held up, the main road over Dunmail Raise was washed away in places and elsewhere piled high with boulders swept down from the fells, while sheep drowned in the floods below Troutbeck Park were found to have been stripped of their wool in the swirling torrents as neatly as if they had been clipped. But the wettest Lake District day ever, according to the records, was November 12th in the previous year, when Seathwaite in Borrowdale recorded 8·03 inches of rain, and, for all I know, ten or twelve inches might have fallen on the high fells.

A more typical November day was one I enjoyed about ten years ago around Ullswater. I remember half a dozen white ducks paddling quietly in line astern past the end of the old tumbledown jetty on the Howtown side, with the sun glinting on the blue, dancing waters of the lake and the houses among the woods on the farther shore, making the perfect colour picture. And there were others just as good—a sheepdog asleep in the morning sun in the porch of a whitewashed farmhouse, a shepherd bringing down his sheep off the fell, a tiny waterfall tumbling over brown rocks, the contrast between the bracken and the bilberry on a far hillside, the rushes around the lonely mountain tarn with the long miles of valley falling away into the distant blues and purple, and white clouds sailing over an up-tilted crag. These rare autumn mornings before the leaves have all been blown away are the days on which to see the Lake District at its colourful best. The distant views seem to have a quiet, dark serenity as if the hills are waiting calmly for the winter snows, while closer at hand the woods and the fellsides are a happy jumble of colour—yellow, gold, rich brown, with here and there a splash of scarlet. It is well to be astir really early these perfect mornings, when the lake is so still that the reflections are perfect, the shadows long and sharp, and the blue woodsmoke rising slowly straight from the cottage chimneys. And the views are finer still if there has been heavy rain the previous day. Then, the atmosphere is so clear that you can see the sea, and the colours have an added freshness. Perhaps a slight mist rises from the river and the intake fields and the patches of damp on the towering crag across the valley glitter in the sunlight like jewels.

One November day I was crunching over snowdrifts three feet deep in the Northern Pennines overlooking the Eden and trying to face into a biting north-east wind. You can get to the summit of Great Dun Fell by car—if you are on official business —by means of the highest road in Britain, for the radio station perched up there is 2,780 feet above sea-level. Men are at work there, day and night throughout the year, providing navigational aid for unseen aircraft, and the low buildings are easily the highest continuously inhabited place in the country. That day the 120-feet-high latticed steel masts were hanging in ice and the station looked like a Siberian outpost, but down in the valley it was a pleasant, sunny autumn day. On our way to the station we watched for a while some aircraft that need neither navigational aid nor engines—the lovely soaring planes of the Lakes Gliding Club. Soundlessly they sailed over the edge of the fell from their launching point, swept gracefully across the gorge, turned, hovered and swooped, and finally crept silently in to land. It was dusk by the time we were down from the high snows and, driving south across the moor, we watched a glorious sunset.

You can watch the salmon and sea trout trying to leap the weir across the River Kent in Kendal on their way to the spawning grounds on many a November day. And one day in Swindale we found half a dozen salmon lazing in a pool the size of a room in a straggling beck more than forty miles from the sea. They lay like blackened, sunken logs in gloomy shallows below a withered rowan, with a rather formidable waterfall a few yards further upstream. Whether this was their next obstacle or whether they had reached the end of their journey we could not say, but certainly they had come a long, long way. It is a fascinating story and even the experts do not know it all. Some tremendous force beyond our comprehension prompts these big fish, somewhere out in the Irish Sea, to risk this long journey to spawn in a remote beck. They say they always come back to the river where they were born, but I cannot vouch for this. But I'm told that once started on their long journey there is no turning back and waterfalls, weirs, and shallows must all be tackled in their turn. The sleek fish looked exhausted and lethargic. We threw in a stone and they slid lazily away and one broke the surface as he slowly turned, showing his long, dark, glistening back. If we had gone at night they would have been even less concerned, for you can then wade into the pools almost among them, and they will not stir. In Scotland the poachers, well aware of this, might go "burning the water" with branches aflame, but in Lakeland the method is more likely to be a hooded torch shone into the likeliest-looking pools and a salmon whipped out on the end of a barbed gaff. Cruel and illegal, certainly, and in any case the flesh not worth eating at this time of the year.

Just before they freed, about six years ago, the last toll road in Westmorland—near Brigsteer—I paid my sixpence to drive this way across the valley. At that time the road was a mile and a half of grass, pot-holes, and puddles across the peaty flats between the low, limestone hills that edge down to the estuary. It could cut nearly four miles off a ten-mile car journey, but few people went this way by car, preferring to save their springs— and their money. Fewer still travelled the stony road driving their stock to market, for, while a sixpenny toll for a motor-car could be accepted on sufferance, a penny for every sheep in a flock of a hundred was only to be considered in the very last resort. When I sounded my horn this time for the gate to be opened I was the first customer for two days, and the first for much longer than that not to complain about the iniquity of it all. "Some of them seem to think I ought to pay them for travelling along the road," confessed the gatekeeper. "And nearly all of them are downright rude, or say they haven't any silver on

Ullswater from Glencoyne Park
Small Water and Haweswater
Middlefell Place, Great Langdale

them." But soon afterwards they took away the gate, had the surface repaired, and freed the road, so that Kendal suddenly became three miles closer to people in the valley of the damson blossom.

Another November day I was at the other end of Westmorland where a roughly hewn obelisk on the lonely moor marks the spot where 300 years ago a King of England halted his army and watered his horses. They drank from a gushing spring that is the source of one of Westmorland's loveliest streams, the Lyvennet, a shy beck that wanders down the limestone fells, through sleepy villages untouched by time, to the Eden. On this same moor, ages before history began, a primitive people built their stone circles, burial mounds, and places of sacrifice, and a thousand years later the Romans laid a straight road for their legions. On a grey, squelching day we found the circles, the road, the stone to mark the passage of a king, the infant river, and, from the summit of the moor, saw the pylons of the electricity grid striding across the fells. The great lattice girders of the later "super" grid, twice as big as these pylons, were originally to go through the quiet valley where lived primitive man, the Romans, and later the Normans who built the church among the trees, But they decided they should go along the busy main road to Scotland and, happily, an unspoiled corner of Westmorland still remains unchanged.

Peep into many a Westmorland home nowadays and you may find, in the place where you might have expected the television set, an awkward-looking hand-loom and, perhaps in another corner, an object more quickly identified as a spinning wheel. Elsewhere such apparatus might have been imported to add a touch of warmth and realism to a room filled with old brass and willow-patterned china, but here they are meant to be used. More people in these parts than you might guess have taken to weaving their own cloth and some of them are even spinning and dyeing their own wool. One farmer's wife—there may be others—has made herself completely self-supporting so far as clothes are concerned. When she requires, for instance, a new winter skirt, she collects the wool from her own Herdwicks, cards it, cleans it, spins it, dyes it with lichen, gorse, or bracken roots, according to the colour desired, weaves it into cloth on her

The Kirkstone road and Red Screes
Winter sunset over Coniston Water

own hand loom, and then makes the garment. This revival in craftsmanship is not confined to the women folk, and I have talked to men proudly wearing suits they have made themselves from balls of wool. In some cases they have made their own looms, too. It is said that the Westmorland archers at Flodden and on many another field wore Kendal Green, and today, in farm and country houses, their descendants are making the same strong cloth and dyeing it with green weed to give it just the right shade.

The dog took the children one sunny November afternoon merrily up the track past the old Applethwaite quarries and away to the top of the Garburn Pass while we followed sedately in the rear. We never took him in the fells in those days—he took us. He seemed to say: "Let me show you the countryside. So much better than your stuffy towns." The day was warm, clear and sunny, but he was not interested in scenery—only in the rabbit holes, the dirty pools, and the birds, who annoyed him. He would dearly love to have chased sheep, too, but after looking longingly at them in the distance remembered his manners. The day before he had been combed and brushed, but he splashed into the first dirty pool and then sat down in it. A moment later he was half-way down a rabbit hole and then away off up the steep bracken towards a grouse, croaking in the heather. On the top of the pass he lay on a rock in the sunshine, tongue out, tail wagging, watching a beetle toiling through the grass jungle. Below us we could just pick out the traffic crawling along the road, and there was the distant sea, and the lakes and the fells standing up around us in the afternoon sunshine, but all he was thinking about was his dinner. It had not been a hard day—he once climbed four mountains between breakfast and dinner—but on the way down he did no more than growl at a huge dog twice his size in the farm yard. Normally he would have been annoyed. But this was years ago. Nowadays, as befits an old dog, he is much more sedate. The fells still beckon, and the spirit is still willing, but his old legs are a bit shaky now.

As I write, at the end of a quiet November, the fells are hidden by cloud and the leaves swirling in half a gale, but, surprisingly, there are reports of travellers trapped overnight in the snow on the pass. Two days ago I was driving along crisp, white roads in the north of the county and admiring the sparkle of sunshine on snowbound hills, so that I longed to get away from humdrum duties and tread the beckoning heights, either of foot or on ski. There might, I thought, be ski-ing—of a sort—somewhere in the Lakeland hills that weekend. Meanwhile on likely days, a watcher from the upper window of a Penrith house trained his telescope on a distant drift high up in the Helvellyn range. When it appeared, long, white, and wide, the winter would be with us, and the Lakeland ski-ing season could be said to have arrived.

12

THE DYING YEAR
December

THE short days of December nearly always provide their con-
trasts in the fell country—bitter days of snow and ice, wild days
of gales and floods, foggy days, too, perhaps, but also quiet,
sunny days with a sleeping countryside moving contentedly
into a new year. On one of these better days when most of England seemed lost in fog I drove up the old road round Potter
Fell and into the Westmorland hills through the sparkling sunshine of a perfect winter afternoon. It was a day for superlatives,
the sky cloudless and blue, the air crisp and clear with views
right across the Lake District, and the day so calm that the
woodsmoke from the cottage chimneys rose straight as the
Borrowdale birches. In the meadows by the river the cattle
stood transfixed like wooden models, bemused perhaps by the
stillness and the sunlight, and at the foot of the hill road two
men in shirt sleeves were laying a hedge and whistling as they
worked. A farmer with two dogs at heel and a gun over his
shoulder came striding down the frozen fellside and two girls
in jodhpurs astride sleek brown ponies trotted out of a side lane.
Near the top of the fell overlooking Longsleddale I found what
I had come for—a long patch of hard snow, tilted at the right
angle and full in the sunshine. My stolen hour of ski-ing was
watched only by my dog and, too soon, it was time to go. For
ten minutes I watched a blazing sun dip down through an
orange sky towards the western hills—the perfect ending to a
lovely winter's day. Already evening had come down in the

valley, but in the hills it was still afternoon. Two silent jet air-craft, golden specks in the late sunlight, made shining trails across the purpling sky, and the sun rimmed the outline of Bow-fell and the Crinkles in gold. I drove down across the crackling pools and the frost-caked road towards the valley and the even-ing lamplight, while a crescent moon shone clear out of a darkening sky.

Sometimes the gales and floods come early in the month, and, well before Christmas, the storms have blown themselves out, the flood waters subsided and a late autumn calm settles over the countryside. Perhaps the day before we had been looking out on flooded fields and listening to the wind shrieking round the house, but the next morning the smoke from the cottages below is drifting slowly across the valley, the ground firm with a first slight dusting of morning frost, and the crocuses, greatly daring, beginning to push their pale spikes through the lawn. These quiet mornings just before the turn of the year, when nature, invigorated and quickened by the storms, seems to be gathering strength to withstand the coming ice and snow, can be unexpectedly rewarding. Often we awake in December to find our little hillside flooded by the orange light of dawn with a golden sun creeping over a distant Yorkshire skyline and a bright moon still shining through the opposite window. A thin mist, floating up from the river, partly hides the woods and the motor road over the fells, but above the greyness the switch-back of the hills rises sharp and inviting. And soon the first sounds come stealing across the valley—the clatter of pails down at the farm, the whirr of a circular saw from the wood-men over the hill, and the farmer with his new hedge cutter tidying up his fences for the winter.

The afternoons are short. Too soon, from a hundred vantage points above the valleys you are watching the dying sun sinking towards the sea, but still catching the snowbound ridges of the mountain backcloth to the north, throwing them into magni-ficent stereoscopic relief. The same sun dances like a shadow-glass on the distant roof of a toy farm far below, and burnishes the glistening trunks of the silver birches. Long shadows creep across the yellowing grass and the trees stand bare and black against grey-flecked skies. Down the valley towards the lake half a dozen wild duck come silently zigzagging above the river, but soon the sun has disappeared and immediately the picture looks colder, while the great northern barrier, with the snows plastered like modelled ivory along the summit ridge, seems much higher. Quickly the last golden glow fades from the river and towards the west the fells are already turning purple in the twilight.

The mountain tarns freeze early and I've found ice-floes on Helvellyn's Red Tarn in December. One day, just before Christmas, we took skates with us when we went for a walk over the top and down Swirral Edge. Patches of snow around the frozen tarn showed clearly how a cautious fox had crept on to the ice, slithered for a few feet, taken fright, and dashed helter-skelter back to the shore. A few yards away a tiny mountain mouse with footprints one-hundredth the size, had, with less ambition, circumnavigated the boulders at the edge and finally gone to earth in a snow-filled hollow. The ice rang like a tuning fork as we tested it, an occasional healthy crack echoed across the silent tarn like a pistol shot, and our blades sang sweetly as we circled in the sunlight. Overhead the pair of ravens who live in the crag at the head of the valley clumsily quartered the tarn as if on sentry-go, and a hundred yards away a kestrel which had seen something on the fell hung poised on beating pinions waiting to strike. In the shallower places where we risked "jump threes" we could see the bottom of the tarn through the black transparent ice and we had the eerie illusion of gliding magically along glass-calm water. An object in the water attracted our attention. We stopped, lay prostrate on the ice, and, with hands cupped round our eyes to keep out the light, could make out a fine, fat trout, motionless, with his nose between two rocks, for all the world as if he were encased in the ice. Although we watched for five minutes he didn't move. We left as the moon came up, and, looking back from near the wall below Striding Edge, saw the tarn shining like a pearl on a purple cushion.

I have written earlier about splendid skating Christmases in Lakeland, and I can think of many other outdoor days in the snow and ice around the turn of the year. There was one, about thirty years ago, when five of us struggled up Coniston Old Man in a blizzard and through snow so deep that every feature of the mountain, including the quarry workings and huts, was completely covered and the tremendous summit cairn of those days buried out of sight. Icicles yards long hung from the crags while Low Water, heaped with great ice floes, looked like some remote corner of the Arctic. Before we got down to our dinner that evening we took off our ice-plated jackets and trousers—there were no anoraks in those days—and stood them up like suits of armour against the walls of the hut. And even more distant Christmas Days, too, when we went out, washed and combed, along quiet lanes to exhibit and exchange presents, or days when we went adventuring in the woods in the thin wintry sunshine to try out new bows and arrows or cowboy outfits. But most outdoor Christmas day memories of Lakeland are of mild, rather misty days, with the few car headlights peering through fog, and a great stillness over a sleeping countryside.

Often it's poor hunting weather in December, either because the snow is too soft, or the frost has killed the scent or it's just too wet and miserable to be out. One year, I remember, huntsmen coming over Kirkstone Pass with a full pack of hounds, lost nearly all in the storm, squelching down into Patterdale, battered and drenched, with only one couple and a terrier or two. The remainder kept turning up all over the Lake District for days afterwards. And the same week lads camping out on Esk Hause in a schoolboy endurance test spent a wretched night holding down a sodden, gale-wrecked tent, after a crawl up the pass, partly on hands and knees, in a wind they had not believed could exist.

It is easy to feel sorry for the sheep, the birds, and the fox-hounds when the weather is miserable on the fells. You may find the sheep, their noses topped with chunks of snow, burrowing down through the drifts only to find the grass frozen hard into the ground. One dark December afternoon I found a foxhound, its lemon-and-white coat hanging in dirt, limping along an upland track above the Duddon towards the highest fells but he would not accompany me down to the farms. He belonged to a pack from a distant valley and no doubt knew where he was going.

Now and again one awakens some December morning to a changed white world with the hills plastered with the first snows of the winter and a new stillness in the air. I managed to seize the chance of the new snow one short afternoon, taking my dog up steep drifts and in and out of little crags to the top of Red Screes looking down on Kirkstone Pass. The white dome of the mountain leaned against a bright blue sky, the sunshine sparkled on the snow and there was hardly enough wind to deflect the smoke from the chimneys of the old inn that crouches solidly on the top of the pass. Three ravens circled the saucer-shaped combe on our left as we trudged up the ridge, with Sambo disappearing now and again in a drift, but these were our only companions and from the summit we looked out across a silent, lonely world where nothing moved except the shadows of the clouds. But the next afternoon two of us were out on skis on Harter Fell with visibility down to a few yards, a biting wind and near-Arctic conditions. Nothing to be seen ahead except the white blanket, dotted here and there with rocks, stretching into the mist, and therefore a need for care, and little in common with the carefree abandon of the sunlit slopes of the travel posters. But wonderful to be on skis in the mountains again with so early a start to the season, although in 1965 we had wonderful ski-ing before the end of November.

Two of us opened the Lake District ski-ing season in the first week of December 1958 with an unadventurous run down the top two miles of the Windermere side of Kirkstone Pass. An attempt on the pass by car had failed because of skidding wheels on an unexpected inch of new, level snow, so we altered plans, backed down the slope, returned home for skis, and attacked the hill on foot. It was a pleasant trudge through the snow to the inn on top of the pass and invigorating, in spite of the protests of softened muscles, to slide down between the stone walls, without much effort, back to the car. So enjoyable, indeed, that we went back for more. A mile further south down the pass there was nothing but half an inch of slush, and a little further south still just dreary, wet roads and a drizzle of rain. But at our little winter sports centre, only five minutes away by car, there was the clean crisp snow all around, an occasional white flurry in the air, and apart from that, just the old brown walls climbing over the fells.

November 1965 was a remarkable month in Lakeland with eighty hours of sunshine in Ambleside and only six inches of rain—half the normal—in Langdale, but the month ended with particularly heavy snowfalls. As a result, December opened with the whole of the countryside, and not only the mountains, completely plastered in snow. Not for very many years has the Lake District looked like this so early in the winter. At first it was an even white blanket, laid down quietly and quickly with no sign of thawing, but then fierce biting winds out of the east, and later, straight down from the Arctic seas, swirled the snows into a maelstrom of fury and the Christmas card scene took on a more sinister appearance. The heroes were the roadmen, struggling through several nights on the high passes against drifts up to twenty feet feep, but, in a few cases, the lorry drivers, by ignoring notices and warnings and crashing on into the blizzard until bogged down or slewed across the road, were incredibly thoughtless. The old tradition—"the mail must get through"—cannot be applied to this reckless behaviour which merely closes the roads to others and leads to a vast amount of unnecessary labour.

Whooper swans landing in a flurry of flapping wings on Brotherswater, a rough-legged buzzard slowly gliding over the Hartsop fields, the fancy white waistcoat of a peregrine peeping out of a high crag, and a fox taking a leisurely afternoon stroll across the fells—all this and more I saw in one short December day some years ago. The swans are often with us for several weeks towards the end of the year, and quarter the whole district very thoroughly in their search for food—one morning, perhaps, on a northern lake, and, in the afternoon, quietly trumpeting on one of the tarns twenty miles to the south. A long spell of severe weather generally brings several of them down from the frozen north. The buzzard, the nearest thing we have got here to a golden eagle, circled the fields very slowly above my head so that I could easily see his feathered legs, his whitish underparts, and his fan-like wings. He was quite contemptuous of my presence, and, having completed his reconnaissance, quietly glided into an oak tree and no doubt sat there until dark. The peregrine—you would be much less likely to see one nowadays—was inaccessible enough and knew it. To complete my day, a gaggle of seven wild geese—greylags, I think—flew in perfect v-shape formation over the hills towards the Solway, with the splendid backcloth of the evening sky behind them, and an occasional, distant croak the only sound.

12

Up to a few years ago only two storm petrels, those friendly
dark brown birds of the ocean, had been sighted in the Lake
District within the last seventy years—one lying dead at Fins-
thwaite and the other flying over Windermere. Then one December day a Westmorland farmer, walking up Scandale, picked
up a third, a damp, lifeless little bundle of feathers lying in the
bracken. The storm petrel lives on the sea, only coming ashore
to breed and then mostly on the islands and, they say, at night.
Obviously this one had been driven ashore by bad weather and
had finally died in a Lake District storm. But for the wideawake
farmer this chance visit to the district would have gone unrecorded. He failed to recognize the bird, sent it along to the
experts, and his discovery now goes into the official records.
More than a hundred of these "rare and accidental visitors" to
the Lake District had been listed by the late Mr. Macpherson,
many of them the result of his own observations over many
years around the Solway Firth. His list includes the frigate
petrel, new to Europe when first reported over the Lake District, the golden eagle, and the Isabelline wheatear. A few of
the birds listed, including some of the mountain birds of prey
and the bittern, chough and wryneck, once bred in the Lake
District, although we can hardly expect the lordly eagle to return to these parts again. He is now listed, however, as a "local"
bird, with three or four confirmed sightings, and at least one
nest was built on a Lake District crag as long ago as 1957, and
a dead eagle found on Shap Fells three years later.

Something like 300 species of birds are reported to have been
seen in and around the Lake District and the latest official
publication forecasts that several birds new to the area are likely
to come up from the south and that others, long extinct, might
return from the north. Two of the most remarkable recent
sightings listed are those of a white stork—the first for fifty
years—and a barred warbler in winter plumage—the first
ever in the district.

We spent one December morning, after the frosts had gone,
planting young trees in my new garden and felt we were planning for posterity. Scots pine, for instance, are perhaps at their
best when fifty years old and tall, dark and rugged against the
sky, so that my three-feet specimens looked very insignificant.

The larches, I knew, would grow very quickly and the birches, too, but the cedars, cypresses and spruces will take many years before they fill their corner. It was difficult to realize that in twenty years time we could be taking our ease in the shade of some of these expensive little sprigs of greenery or even cutting them down for timber. For there's one nursery high up in the Westmorland hills, near Ravenstonedale, in as exposed a place as you could find, where tens of thousands of young trees are sprouting merrily within a high shelter belt of forest trees planted only about fifteen years ago. So we might well live to see the fruits of our labours. So far, one of my most encouraging successes, on a bare north-facing slope 500 feet up, has been the weeping willow. In its three years in my garden it has been almost killed by sodium chlorate washed down the bank into its roots and then, a little later, stripped down to a bare stick by invading, hungry cows, but seems to have thrived on the treatment and is now in full vigorous growth, trailing its delicate leaves over several square yards of garden. An almond tree, also half consumed by cattle, is also enjoying a new lease of life. Indeed, some forestry men tell me that the less you fuss over a tree the better it will grow. Which could well be true, for young birches, carefully transplanted into compost, well-rotted manure, and bone meal, have failed to survive, while a sprig of oak heeled into a pile of builders' rubble is now bursting with life each summer while twigs of flowering cherry stuck unceremoniously into untilled soil are now promising young trees.

Many years ago, when I lived far away from Lakeland for quite a long time, I used to drive home hot-foot to the fell country each Christmas time, sighing for a sight of the hills and hungry for the smell of woodsmoke and roast pork. Our Christmases must have changed since those days for nearly always, I seem to remember, I came up through the snow. One year I was stuck for a time in snow drifts near Levens Bridge and on another Christmas Eve I remember sliding backwards in my car down a snowbound hill somewhere near Newton on my way to Newby Bridge. It was sometimes quite an adventure even to reach Lakeland in those days for the district—even a short generation ago—seemed to have about it a wonderful feeling of remoteness in wintertime. The inn at the top of

Kirkstone, for instance, always seemed to be "cut off" from the outside world and if one got fairly into the centre of Lakeland there was always the chance that one might not get out again so easily. The roads, of course, were not so good, road maintenance not so important as it is today, and the winters were more severe.

We always got into the fells at Christmas time—Boxing Day was the great day for this—and sometimes the skating was very good or we had sport in ice-filled gullies. Sometimes we looked in at a foxhunt, but we never made a day of it as some people do. We thought we had better things to do. I may be wrong, but I have the impression that more of the hotels were open in Lakeland during Christmas some years ago. People would make up big parties to eat out, providing their own entertainment, which was rather a different sort of thing from the organized Christmas holiday arrangements made nowadays by some of the larger hotels. We used to take over a sort of village hall for a huge party of family and friends, with presents for the children, music, dancing, games and always more than enough to eat. Music was always an important feature of Christmas. On at least one evening during the short holiday there was singing round the piano, for everybody either sang or played. We used to go right through all the carols, and then the Scottish Students Song Book, finishing up with extracts from *Messiah* or *Judas Maccabaeus*. Nowadays one sits round the television watching other people making music.

Sometimes we went carol singing on Christmas Eve outside the houses of our friends—by invitation. These were rather serious affairs for we rather prided ourselves on our music making. There would be a conductor and perhaps a trumpet and a cornet or even a trombone. We learned the different voices and scorned merely to sing in unison. Today, radio and television have taken over our carol singing and there are not nearly so many bands and choirs in the towns and villages on Christmas Eve. One of the great joys of Christmas used to be listening to the village bands and choirs on Christmas morning. Many a time I have seen them standing in the snow underneath the street lights, or have lain in bed on a frosty morning listening to the old sweet tunes.

There's no delivery of mail and parcels on Christmas morning nowadays, but many years ago the arrival in snowbound Lakeland of the coaches laden with Christmas mail must have been an exciting occasion. The late W. T. Palmer, who came of a coaching family, used to write about these old days. The drivers wore the vermilion jackets of the Royal Mail and the coaches drawn by four horses would be crowded with holidaymakers who had travelled up from the south for a real Lakeland Christmas. Sometimes the mail had to come through deep snow over the passes with a postilion on the leaders, and it was said that no matter how deep the snow or how bad the weather the horses would never swerve one foot from their place on the unseen road below the drifts. The whisky, it is also said, used to flow like water around the postmen who brought the mail to the villages, but I've no doubt they deserved it. At one time it was a four and a half days' journey from Manchester to London but later the Edinburgh mail ran the 400 miles from London in forty hours dead. Sometimes the coach guards used to bring turkeys and other Christmas fare from the big markets and make good profit from the Lakeland folk.

It must have been a wonderful sight to see the coach lamps shining through the morning mist as the spanking crimson coaches came bowling along the lake shores towards the villages with the Christmas mail on board, and to hear the driver, well wrapped up against the cold, sounding his yard-long coaching horn and awakening the echoes across the valley. These are the sort of Christmases we might have read about or even some of us remember. It cannot be the same today, but some of the old atmosphere is still there in Lakeland if you look for it.

And so the year ends as it has begun—the fells flecked with snow, a smudge of grey smoke hanging above the little towns and villages, the skies angry with their message of storms to come, but the earth asleep. We can see there are two different worlds—the quiet of the dales with the first bulbs sprouting in the garden borders and the fields either sodden or frozen hard, and the winter of the mountain tops with the snow whirling off the cornices and perhaps the crags hanging in ice. You might get almost a balmy December day in the valley and yet see plumes of snow blown off the highest peaks. But for the real lover of the Lake Country there can be joy on any day, no matter what the weather; always something new to see, or to experience, always something to learn. There are no bad days in Lakeland, although there may be uncomfortable ones. In half an hour you can get away into this other world, away from motor-cars and noise and speed and worry, and, at most turns of the year in Lakeland, tread unmarked snows or wander along unpeopled tracks. Yesterday, from the top of a Westmorland hill, I could see little but miles of snow and the valley below, unseen behind a hummock, might be a day's march away. I could see Scotland —forty miles away across the Solway—but not a living thing. The crags below my feet, friendly in summer, looked menacing in their shadowed, slippery steepness but the storms had also changed each long blade of grass about the summit into a tinkling, fairy mushroom of ice—shelters, perhaps, for the mountain sprites.

More and more people are learning something about this winter world and many, many more discovering the delights of spring, summer and autumn in the hills. Within the space of a few years many things have changed. Mountain tops where you might once have found summer solidude are now traversed by caravans of walkers; crags, once the preserve of the few, have become so popular that you might have to queue up for your climb; the roads over the passes become crowded at weekends, and main roads into the National Park are becoming speed tracks. But even on a sunny August Monday, a man with his wits about him may still seek out his private waterfall or couch of bilberry and dream away a long afternoon without seeing, or being spotted by, a soul. But you have to know where to go. June, July, and August will always be crowded months in the Lake District, even if they include no Bank Holidays, and October is often a worthwhile holiday time. But the connoisseur will still avoid the popular months and come to the fell country when the crowds have gone, the villages back to their normal way of life, and the distant views long and clear.

The highway through the Lake District, past Wordsworth's home, has been "improved", with by-passes and almost motorway dimensions planned, so that nothing can stand in the way of the Midlands motorist anxious to reach the shrine in an easy morning's run. You could not wish for a tidier or more efficient job, but the charm of the old twisting road, with a different scene around every bend, has already gone. Today, in effect, you step off a motorway to climb up into the fells whereas in more leisured days half the fun was the joy of arriving. First there was the sight of rising pastures above the limestone outcrops, a slow progress along leafy lanes between old stone walls, a cheery word from a dalesman at his cottage door or a huntsman out with his hounds and then, suddenly, sunlight sparkling on a corner of a lake and the hills peeping over the trees. Men, they say, can kill the things they love, and mass tourism is threatening the Lake District, but although the popular places may become more popular and some old values change, the fells are not likely to alter much in the next hundred years. There will still be places when you and I are gone where a man can discover beauty and solitude and adventure, or find his soul uplifted or even be reborn. Places where a man may be humbled among the finest gifts of Nature and see himself for what he is.

INDEX